IS-0366.a - Planning for the Needs of Children in Disasters

By

Fema

12/9/2015

IS-0366.a - Planning for the Needs of Children in Disasters

Table of Contents:

Lesson 1: Course Overview

Course Overview

The purpose of this course is to provide the students with the tools and confidence to become more effective in planning and meeting the unique needs that arise among children as a result of a disaster or emergency.

Much of the information you will learn in this course is based upon a document titled "The Unique Needs of Children in Emergencies: A Guide for the Inclusion of Children in Emergency Operations Plans," published by Save the Children.

The target audience for this course is local and state emergency managers and planners. Other individuals or groups that may benefit from taking this course including those directly involved with meeting the needs of children, such as the following:

- Judges and other members of the State, county, and local governmental legal system
- Voluntary Organizations Active in Disasters (VOADs), faith-based organizations and other non-profits
- Child service agencies
- Child care providers
- Schools

At the conclusion of this course, you will be able to revise an emergency operations plan for your community or organization to effectively address the unique needs of children in disasters.

This course is designed to help accomplish the goals and priorities of FEMA:

FEMA's mission is to support our citizens and first responders to ensure that as a nation we work together to build, sustain, and improve our capability to prepare for, protect against, respond to, recover from, and mitigate all hazards.

Screen Features

Selectable Item	Screen Feature
Course Menu	Click on the **Course Menu** button to access the menu listing all lessons of this course. You can select any of the lessons from this menu by simply clicking on the lesson title.
Help	Click on the **Help** button to review guidance and troubleshooting advice regarding navigating through the course.
Glossary	Click on the **Glossary** button to look up key definitions and acronyms.
Progress	Track your progress by looking at the **Progress** bar at the top right of each screen. To see a numeric display, roll your mouse over the Progress bar area.
Instruction	Follow the bolded green instructions that appear on each screen in order to proceed to the next screen or complete a Knowledge Review or Activity.
Back and Next	

Click on the **Back** or the **Next** buttons at the top and bottom of screens to move backward or forward in the lesson. **Note:** If the **Next** button is **dimmed**, you must complete an activity before you can proceed in the lesson.

Navigating Using Your Keyboard

Below are instructions for navigating through the course using your keyboard.

- Use the "Tab" key to move forward through each screen's navigation buttons and hyperlinks, or "Shift" + "Tab" to move backwards. A box surrounds the button that is currently selected.

- Press "Enter" to select a navigation button or hyperlink.

- Use the arrow keys to select answers for multiple-choice review questions or self-assessment checklists. Then tab to the "Submit" button and press "Enter" to complete a Knowledge Review or Self-Assessment.

- **Warning:** Repeatedly pressing "Tab" beyond the number of selections on the screen may cause the keyboard to lock up. Use "Ctrl" + "Tab" to deselect an element or reset to the beginning of a screen's navigation links (most often needed for screens with animations or media).

- JAWS assistive technology users can press the Ctrl key to quiet the screen reader while the course audio plays

Course Features

Except for this lesson and the Resources Toolkit that comes at the end of the course, every lesson begins and ends with a movie that tells a story about children in disasters. To view these movies, please ensure that you have the latest version of Flash player installed and that your speakers are on. After you view the movie, you will be asked a related question about planning for the needs of children in **your community**.

In addition to these open-ended questions, you will be asked **knowledge review** questions to assess your understanding of the material. Supplemental information and examples related to the content are provided. The Resources Toolkit, contains checklists and other useful information.

"Your Community"

In each lesson, you will be asked to list actions already being taken in your community to provide for the unique needs of children. After you have progressed through the lesson, you will be asked to brainstorm other actions that your community could take to better meet these needs, based on what you learned.

After typing your response to each of these questions, it is recommended that you print your answer for future reference during emergency operations planning in your community.

Knowledge Reviews

"Knowledge Review" screens provide activities to help review the content covered in the course. Green text at the bottom of the screen provides instructions on how to complete each activity. A box will appear with feedback about the choices selected. After reading the feedback, click the Continue button to proceed.

Receiving Credit

To receive credit for this course, you must:

- **Complete all of the lessons.** Each lesson will take between 10 and 50 minutes to complete. It is important to allow enough time to complete the course in its entirety.
- Check the length of the lesson on the overview screen.
  Remember . . . YOU MUST COMPLETE THE ENTIRE COURSE TO RECEIVE CREDIT. If you have to leave the course, do not exit from the course or close your browser. If you exit from the course, you will need to start that lesson over again.
- **Pass the final exam.** The last screen provides instructions on how to complete the Final Exam.

Lesson Summary

This completes this lesson. In this lesson you learned:

- What this course is about
- How to complete this course
- How to receive credit for this independent study course

The remainder of this course will focus on considerations for revising an emergency operations plan for your community or organization so you can effectively plan for the unique needs of children in disasters.

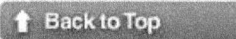 Back to Top

Lesson 2: Unique Needs of Children in Disasters

Lesson Overview

The American Academy of Pediatrics has established that children have unique physical and emotional needs when a disaster strikes. In addition to being placed at an increased risk of physical harm, children respond to illness, injury, and treatment differently than adults do. They also rely on stable routines in their daily lives, and when a disaster occurs, the drastic changes to their known world not only endanger their safety, but also greatly frighten them. To ensure the physical security and emotional stability of children in disasters, communities must customize their emergency planning efforts.

This lesson will discuss the unique needs of children in disasters as they relate to physical security and emotional stability, and how preserving family unity during an emergency can help to meet these needs.

Upon completion of this lesson you will be able to:

- Identify types of threats to the physical security of children in disasters.
- Describe the emotional impact a disaster may have on a child.
- Describe the critical role of the family to children in a disaster.

The Children of Katrina and Rita

Audio Transcript

Charles and Lisa were at their New Orleans home with five of their six children when Hurricane Katrina struck. Their three-year-old daughter, Cortez, was in another part of the city with her godmother.

As flood waters rose around their home, the family was rescued by boat. Four days later, the family was evacuated to Houston. Though Charles and Lisa constantly watched the crowds for their daughter, there was no sign of little Cortez.

Cortez's parents had no way of knowing she had survived the storm. Seeking higher ground, her godmother had taken her into a hotel. After being rescued by helicopter, they were evacuated to Atlanta.

During and after Hurricanes Katrina and Rita, over 411,000 people were evacuated from the Gulf Coast area. They were scattered across the nation without accurate records to track where they were being sent.

Cortez' godmother tried desperately for many months to contact the little girl's parents. All the while, Charles and Lisa wondered if they would ever see their daughter again.

Unfortunately, this story is not unique. 5,192 children were reported as missing or displaced as a result of Hurricanes Katrina and Rita.

Source: Press Release, "National Center for Missing & Exploited Children Reunites Last Missing Child Separated by Hurricane Katrina and Rita." March 17, 2006.

Protecting Children During Disasters

The emergency operations plan for your community or organization must consider the physical and emotional dangers to children during a disaster and include appropriate prevention and mitigation methods.

Save the Children, a charitable organization dedicated to helping children in need, has identified that children in disaster areas require protection from:

Physical Harm

Because of the nature of disasters, children are at an increased risk for physical harm from many dangers:

- Injury from building collapse, motor vehicle crashes, or debris.
- Injury or assault in an evacuation shelter.
- Infection from spilled chemicals or pollutants in standing water.
- Ingestion of spoiled food or polluted water.

- Extended periods without proper nutrition or water.
- Exposure to inclement weather (hot or cold).
- Attack by feral animals.
- Existing or chronic illness aggravated by disruption in medical attention.
- Lack of access to appropriate health care professionals, medicine and equipment.

Exploitation and Gender-based Violence

During emergency situations, children are especially vulnerable to sexual violence and other means of exploitation, particularly when they are separated from their families or otherwise displaced, such as when evacuated to a large shelter.

Psychosocial Distress

Because the physical needs of disaster victims are generally the focus of relief efforts, there is a danger of overlooking the emotional well-being of children who are subjected to stressful situations during an emergency. Communities must consider ways of reducing psychological and social distress during disasters, while fostering hope and confidence in children.

Recruitment into Gangs

Children naturally seek acceptance and belonging, and during times of crisis, they can be particularly susceptible to recruitment by gangs.

Family Separation

When an emergency occurs, families are often separated because they cannot safely get to each other's location. In large disasters involving evacuation, families may be separated for extended periods.

Abuses Related to Evacuation

Children placed in temporary homes may be subject to abuse at the hands of those who are supposed to be taking care of them. Children evacuated to shelters may be at risk of violence and emotional trauma due to the nature of the mixed population at the shelter. Besides these kinds of abuse, children may also suffer unintentional neglect of their medical needs because basic health services may not be available.

Denial of Children's Access to Quality Education

Often during emergencies, even when a school building is left intact by the disaster, the building may be used as a temporary shelter, and other issues such as loss of power may prevent the school from operating.

The Emotional Impact of Disaster

Crisis situations are especially difficult for children emotionally. Often, the perception that children are naturally resilient causes people to expect them to simply bounce back from a disaster. However, children are profoundly affected by upheaval in their worlds and need opportunities to share their concerns with other children and caring adults in order to recover from and cope with the effects of a disaster.

Indonesian Tsunami's Impact on Children

Following the tsunami of December 2004, Save the Children asked over 500 parents and caregivers in Aceh Province, Indonesia to describe how their children's attitudes and behaviors changed as a result of the tsunami.

The following answers were the most common:

- Children cannot sleep and are afraid to close their eyes at night.
- They don't want to go near the ocean.
- Some are afraid to go back to schools that were damaged.
- Many have lost their self-confidence.
- Some become upset or cry when they hear loud noises.
- Many have bad dreams.

Parents said their children's worst fears were that the tsunami would happen again and that they would be separated from their parents.

Helping Children Cope with Emotions

Save the Children offers community-based recovery and resilience-building programs for children and their caregivers. These workshops use cooperative games and structured play, expressive exercises, and art activities to help children:

- Rebuild a sense of safety and normalcy.
- Express their thoughts and feelings about their experiences.
- Strengthen resilience, or coping skills.
- Build positive relationships with peers and caregivers.

These workshops are also known as psychosocial programs because they address children's personal, emotional, and social needs.

Ten Tips to Help Children Cope with Disaster

Children are often deeply affected by what they see and hear during and after an emergency. During major disasters, children across the country may be frightened by media reports of the destruction, even if their families were not in harm's way.

Concerned about the emotional well-being of their children, many parents, teachers, grandparents and care-givers look for advice on how to respond to questions from children about disasters.

The following ten tips are listed below for responding to emergencies and crises in the United States and internationally and can be used as a guide for adults to support children through times of crisis.

- Hug your children often and comfort them.
- Listen to children carefully and give them opportunities to talk about what happened.
- Limit TV time — news and pictures can be frightening.
- Watch for changes in your children's behavior. If your child continues to display disruptions in eating, sleeping or daily activities, or if you as the caregiver feel uncomfortable or concerned, seek assistance from a mental health professional.
- Be patient and understanding — your children might still be upset or frightened.
- Give your children extra time and attention.
- Use positive behavior and language around your children.
- Take care of yourself and do healthy things to relax. Try to get enough rest.
- Help your children return to school, normal activities and routines.
- Encourage children to volunteer and help others.

Source: Save the Children. (2014). *How to help children cope with disasters: 10 tips from Save the Children* ("Get Ready. Get Safe." campaign). Available from http://www.savethechildren.org/atf/cf/%7B9def2ebe-10ae-432c-9bd0-df91d2eba74a%7D/GRGS_10_TIPS_FOR_COPING.PDF

Preserving Family Unity

Being separated from loved ones during an emergency is a frightening situation for anyone, but it is especially traumatic and dangerous for children. Planning for ways to preserve family unity is the most important step you can take to provide for the physical safety and emotional stability of children in disasters.

Children can become separated from their families in many situations, including:

- During an evacuation.
- At emergency shelters.
- While at school or a child care facility.
- While on a school trip out of town.
- While at summer camp or after-school activities.
- While being treated at a hospital or medical clinic.
- While visiting friends or relatives away from home
- While at the store, at the movies, or other location.

The emergency operations plan for your community or organization should include procedures for identifying children who have been separated from their families and reuniting the families as soon, and as carefully, as possible.

Toolkit to Preserve Family Unity

The Centers for Disease Control and Prevention (CDC) has developed five critical steps to help shelters, hospitals, and medical clinics prevent separation of children from their families and identify those who have already been separated. These steps have also been adopted by Save the Children.

5 Critical Steps to Preserve Family Unity During Emergencies

- Survey all children to identify children who are not accompanied by an adult who is supervising them.
- Place an identification bracelet on the child that matches a supervising adult, if available.
- Report all unaccompanied children to the emergency operations center and the NCMEC (National Center for Missing and Exploited Children).
- Send a complete list of unaccompanied children to local emergency management officials.
- Have a physician, preferably a pediatrician; conduct a social and health screening of the child and the supervising adult.

The Children of Katrina and Rita

Video Transcript

In the months following Hurricanes Katrina and Rita, FEMA partnered with the National Center for Missing & Exploited Children and other agencies to locate the missing children so they could be reunited with their families.

Day by day, week by week, as the newspapers reported stories of missing children being returned home, Charles and Lisa waited to hear the fate of their daughter. Months went by. Cortez's fourth birthday came and went. Her family hoped for the best while fearing the worst.

Finally, some investigative work paid off. With the help of the U.S. Postal Inspection Service, the National Center for Missing & Exploited Children was able to track down Cortez's godmother through a previous employer and locate her family in Georgia. Charles and Lisa's little girl was coming home.

Little Cortez, now four years old, was reunited with her parents, brothers, and sisters on March 16, 2006, more than six months after the disaster. Finally, the last of Katrina and Rita's missing children had been found.

Lesson Summary

This completes this lesson. In this lesson you learned:

- Types of threats to the physical security of children in disasters.
- The emotional impact a disaster may have on a child.
- The critical role of the family to children in a disaster.

When developing the emergency operations plan, your community or organization must consider ways to protect children from physical harm and ensure that appropriate medical care is available for children injured in disasters. Your plan should also address methods for enhancing children's emotional stability because it can be easily disrupted by a disaster event. Programs are available to help children and caregivers plan for disasters and cope with them after an event occurs.

Family unity is critical to children's physical security and emotional stability. Steps must be taken before a disaster to reduce the chances that families will be separated and ensure that, if they are separated, the families are reunited in a timely and careful manner.

Lesson 3: Critical Components of a Child's World

Lesson Overview

The effect of disaster on a community's critical infrastructure, such as roads, water supplies, power supplies, and communication systems, is often at the forefront of emergency operations planning. When planning for the unique needs of children in disasters, you should also consider critical components of a child's world. In this lesson, you will learn the importance of the people, facilities, and services that make up a child's infrastructure.

Upon completion of this lesson, you will be able to:

- Explain the importance of various components of a community's infrastructure and facilities that support its children.
- Identify legal considerations when caring for children in disasters.

Child Care: The Backbone of the Community

Audio Transcript

Chevron Pascagoula refinery has been operating in Jackson County, Mississippi, for over 40 years and is a vital part of the community.

When Hurricane Katrina struck the Gulf Coast, Chevron leadership knew that it was important to reopen the refinery as quickly as possible – not merely to support the company's bottom line, but to support the restoration and recovery of the community.
For families to begin rebuilding their lives in Jackson County, they needed to go back to work.

However, approximately 70% of child care centers in Jackson County were either totally destroyed by the storm or in need of repairs before they could reopen.
Without child care, parents were unable to return to work, and without people working, the local economy could not recover.

Because child care was not on the government's list of critical services, it was not immediately eligible for federal disaster aid.

Throughout the coastal counties in Mississippi, 3 out of 4 children who had a space in a child care program before Hurricane Katrina had no place to go after the storm.

Critical Components of a Child's World

Because stable routines are critical to the physical and emotional well-being of a child, an emergency operations plan must consider ways to prevent or minimize disruption to a child's routine during and after a disaster.

Much of a child's everyday routine is shaped by:

- Families
- Child care providers
- Schools
- Classmates and friends
- Child social services.

Family as Critical Infrastructure for Children

The first means of accounting for children in disasters is through the family. Family leaders will make the decisions about whether to evacuate in the face of an impending disaster, whether to seek shelter, and how to provide safety and care for the children.

Families come in all shapes and sizes, and you should be familiar with the various legal and societal definitions of a family.

In today's society, children live in families that are headed by:

- Two parents
- A single parent
- Grandparent(s)
- Guardian(s)
- Foster parent(s)
- Sibling(s).

Also, some children may be homeless, with or without parental supervision.

Whatever the family unit, emergency managers must consider ways to keep families together when planning for disasters, in order to maintain continuity in a child's life and ensure that the child is properly cared for.

Keeping Families Together During Evacuation

After Hurricane Katrina, emergency management officials in New Orleans recognized the need for a city-assisted evacuation plan to help residents who do not have the means to evacuate on their own. According to the first draft of the plan, all residents with special medical needs were to be evacuated separately from those without special medical needs. However, this policy could have resulted in separation of families if this oversight in planning had not been caught by plan reviewers.

For example, if a woman in a wheelchair reports for evacuation accompanied by her grandson for whom she is guardian, a plan that calls for separate evacuation of people with special medical needs would send the grandmother to one location and her grandson to another.

The evacuation plan for New Orleans was later revised to include procedures to ensure family unity during evacuation. If one family member has special medical needs, the entire family is evacuated together.

Child Care as Critical Infrastructure for Children

Child care is a critical part of a community's infrastructure. The child care industry has a large impact on the economy because it provides employment and generates revenue through purchases made by the employees. A study by the Louisiana Department of Social Services found that child care businesses in the state employ approximately 20% more workers than the oil and gas extraction industry.

In addition to being necessary for a community's economy, child care is a necessary component of day-to-day life for many families. Without child care facilities, parents may be unable to go to work. According to the National Association of Child Care Resource and Referral Agencies (NACCRA), "nearly two-thirds of children under the age of six, or 11.6 million children are routinely cared for by someone other than their working parents each day." These child care providers become an important part of the daily life of the children they serve.

Community emergency operations plans must consider child care as necessary both to the economic stability of the community and to the emotional stability of the community's children. If child care facilities are damaged in a disaster, it can have devastating effects to the community's economy, and the disruption in the daily routine can be quite traumatic to children.

Child Care Resource and Referral Agencies

Community-based Child Care Resource and Referral Agencies (CCR&Rs) can be a vital resource for emergency planning, mitigation, response, and recovery. These agencies can:

- Help child care programs and individual providers prepare for potential disasters.
- Represent the child care community in local, state, regional, and national disaster planning.
- Inform and help parents before, during, and after disasters.
- Aid in setting up temporary child care arrangements for first responders' families after a disaster.
- Help child care providers protect their child care businesses during and after disasters.
- Help displaced providers become reemployed and recruiting providers to replace those lost.
- Help restore the quantity and quality of child care in a community after a disaster.
- Coordinate charitable contributions to child care providers and programs following a disaster.
- Protect CCR&R assets during disasters so the agency can continue to serve the community.
- Check with your local first responders for more information.

Schools as Critical Infrastructure for Children

Although most communities include school buildings as potential shelters in their emergency planning efforts, schools must also be considered as critical components of a child's world. The importance of schools in a child's life cannot be emphasized enough. Children between the ages of five and eighteen spend approximately 25% of their waking hours in school, and much of their attitudes are shaped by the experiences and relationships they have in school. Schools provide a structured environment, positive role models, and nutritious meals that some children may lack at home.

Teachers and counselors can help shape a child's perception of what impact a disaster can have on them and how to cope with these impacts. Disaster preparedness curriculum is available to help teach children how to prepare for and respond to disasters and other emergencies.

Masters of Disaster Curriculum

The *Masters of Disaster* curriculum materials, from the American Red Cross, meet national educational standards and can be used to help reduce children's anxiety about unknown aspects of disasters and tragic events.

STEP: Student Tools for Emergency Planning

The STEP program empowers students to encourage their families to make their own emergency kits and communications plans. The program was developed as a joint effort between state emergency management agencies and FEMA and was designed with teachers in mind; it offers ready-to-teach preparedness lessons that do not require a great deal of classroom time. The STEP program has been piloted with much success in Region 1.

Including Schools in Emergency Operations Planning

Including schools in emergency operations planning is essential to provide for the unique needs of children in disasters. School personnel are responsible for the physical safety of children when they are in school and must establish school evacuation, shelter-in-place, and lock-down procedures and conduct regular drills with children. The school administrators should communicate to the parents and guardians how the school will function should a disaster event occur during a school day, as well as how and when parents and guardians can remove the children from the school.

Emergency managers must also be aware of the plans and procedures schools use for evacuation, shelter-in-place, and lock-down, and should work closely with the school system in designing, implementing, and exercising these plans. School nurses and health consultants should be included in disaster planning efforts and should coordinate with local health departments and Emergency Medical Services (EMS) units.

What School Administrators Can Do

Save the Children recommends the following activities to prepare schools and school children for disasters:

- Establish partnerships with all outside groups that will have an impact on your schools during and after an incident.
- Become involved with the communities emergency operations planning process.
- Use internal resources to network externally and assist in the district's emergency planning. For example, a school nurse can act as a liaison with the public health sector, and a school psychologist can work with local mental health resources.
- Establish pre-disaster agreements between schools and/or facilities to temporarily house children until they can be released to parents/guardians.
- Conduct disaster drills in schools.
- Develop procedures for parent/student reunification.
- Involve parents and guardians in school-based emergency operations planning efforts.
- Plan with local community groups how to place children who have not been picked up after a local disaster.
- Develop procedures for establishing instant classrooms (including staff, supplies and appropriate curricula) within close proximity to shelter locations, in the event that schools are damaged, destroyed or converted into community shelters.
- Develop procedures for the replacement of damaged or destroyed educational materials.
- Ensure that all students' educational records are backed up in a safe, offsite location.
- Incorporate materials on the hazards that affect the community in regular curricula.
- Plan for the replacement of teachers and child care personnel who will leave to deal with their own disaster consequences.
- Assist educators in returning to work, and have a system in place to recruit and hire additional staff as needed.
- Work with the district social services office/coordinator to provide training for educators in supporting children faced with stress and potentially more serious psychological problems, including anxiety, depression, behavioral problems, and Post Traumatic Stress Disorder (PTSD), and appropriate responses and referrals.
- With the district social services office/coordinator, provide support for teachers facing stress.

Care for the Caregiver

After a disaster occurs, it is helpful for children to return to school where their attendance and behaviors can be monitored, although they should not be rushed into ordinary routines before they are ready. Children should be given time to talk about how they feel, whether in private sessions with the school counselor or in group sessions where they can discuss the event with their peers. It may also be helpful for the school to hold a workshop for parents about how to help their children cope with the disaster.

While providing support for the children during this recovery period, teachers, counselors, administrators, and school nurses must be encouraged to take care of themselves as well. They may need to form or join support groups to discuss their reactions and deal with the stresses associated with the disaster, as well as to share strategies and best practices for helping the students. If needed, school personnel should be allowed time to care for personal injuries and address any damage that occurred to their property.

Save the Children has developed a one-day workshop called Journey of Hope designed to support teachers, administrators, parents, and child care providers in efforts to process recent events, cope with current challenges, and realize healthier futures.

Journey of Hope

Addressing their own needs for self-care and strengthening community cohesion increases the capacity of caregivers to be fully present and attentive to the needs of children. Journey of Hope provides the opportunity for teachers and parents to understand the journey of their own lives through and beyond the recent disaster. The model draws on the ideas and experiences of teachers, school social workers, administrators and others working for children's well-being.

Journey of Hope gathers participants around a circle in order to build trust and a sense of community. Activities incorporate creative methods including silent storytelling, music, and cooperative games adapted for adults, as well as practical knowledge and skills for self-care. The workshop facilitates the creation of a safe space for teachers and other caregivers in:

- Building trust and community
- Understanding reactions to stress and enhancing skills for coping
- Collective processing of grief and loss
- Identifying and amplifying community strengths and assets
- Collaborative planning for future community-led action and support.

The aim is to provide space for individual and group reflection of their journey, and to develop a sustainable plan for strengthening the school and living community.

Classmates and Friends as Critical Infrastructure for Children

Children require strong emotional support not only from their families, teachers, and other caregivers, but also from their peers. Separation from classmates and friends can be very difficult for a child during and after a disaster. Once reunited, classmates and friends can support each other in dealing with the emotional and psychological impacts of the disaster.

Emergency planners must consider ways to return children to daily activities that involve social interaction after a disaster strikes. Upon return to school or child care, children should be encouraged to work together in small groups to strengthen peer relationships, which can help children cope with stress by allowing them to reconnect with the relationships they have formed with other children.

Special Considerations for Displaced Children

When families are forced to relocate as a result of a disaster, the displaced children should be placed into schools with local children instead of being grouped together with other displaced children. This provides them a sense of normalcy and stability while allowing them to focus on the future.

At the same time, children should be allowed to retain their connections with friends and other familiar people. The National Association of School Psychologists recommends the following ways to help children adjust to relocation:

- Provide opportunities for children to see friends.
- Bring personal items that the child values when staying in temporary housing.
- Establish some daily routines so the child has a sense of what to expect.
- Provide opportunities for children to share their ideas and listen carefully to their concerns or fears.
- Be sensitive to the disruption that relocation may cause and be responsive to the child's needs.
- Consider the developmental level and unique experiences of each child.

Child Social Services as Critical Infrastructure for Children

Social services agencies play a key role in the lives of many children in a community, including foster children, orphans, and other at-risk children. Understanding these roles and responsibilities is critical for emergency managers when planning for disaster events, whether your community is directly affected by a disaster or is hosting families who have been evacuated from a disaster area.

Save the Children recommends that Social Services be involved with the following activities when planning to meet the needs of children in disasters:

- Develop guardianship protocols to guide the care of children separated from their parents at shelters, schools, or child care facilities.
- Develop procedures for placement of children during disaster and terrorist events in case of injured or deceased family members.
- Establish pre-disaster agreements between facilities that care for children and mass care organizations that dictate what shelters children will be brought to in emergencies and the likely needs of those children.
- Develop policies and procedures for the ongoing care of children who are separated from their parents and are unable to be quickly reunited, including transportation, supervision, shelter, care, and nutrition.
- Assist all facilities that care for children with planning for shelter-in-place scenarios.

What Child Social Services Can Do During Response

- Identify, track, and address the needs of sheltered special needs children.
- Provide children with a sense of normalcy as soon as possible after the critical phase of the emergency has ended.
- Establish safe play areas in all shelters to foster natural childhood development.
- Provide communication assistance for children who require it (e.g., children who do not speak English, children with speech or sensory disabilities).
- Assist in the social integration of children, especially those who are separated from their families and friends or who are otherwise displaced.
- Minimize parent/child or guardian/child separation.
- Maintain strong communication with parents/guardians about the well-being of their children (while the children are in supervised care and while they are with their parents/guardians), to help parents identify and track potential problems.
- Document all significant activities.
- Apply a family-centered approach after a disaster that includes assessment, early intervention, and treatment with parents, guardians and primary caregivers.
- Ensure that transient children (children of tourists, non-residents in facilities including camps and boarding schools) are identified, tracked and cared for.

Emergency Managers and Social Services Working Together for Children

In the aftermath of Hurricane Katrina, 32 states across the country received Federal disaster assistance from FEMA and other agencies to help pay for hosting Katrina evacuees that were displaced to their community. Emergency managers in these host communities worked closely with social services agencies to help displaced children in their care.

Considerations for Emergency Operations Planning

Many questions may arise during a disaster and must be taken into consideration during your planning efforts. Because laws differ from state to state, you must consider the following issues as they apply in your community:

- For unaccompanied children during a disaster, consent is not needed to treat for a life- or limb-threatening situation. Is parental consent needed to treat a child victim with minor injuries? With psychological injuries?
- Is parental consent required to decontaminate an unaccompanied child? What if the child is asymptomatic? What if the child is refusing?
- What medical or social information can be released, and to whom, during a disaster?
- What are your unidentified patient locator protocols? Check Health Insurance Portability and Accountability Act (HIPAA) rules and your legal counsel concerning these protocols, such as posting photographs of unidentified children.
- To whom can children be released? If being released to someone other than the parent or caregiver, what permission or information is needed? What is your protocol for releasing children if no legal guardian or parent can be found or if no permission document is provided?

Involving the Legal System

Engaging the legal system in the community is one way emergency managers can appropriately deal with legal issues regarding at-risk children in disasters. The legal system could:

- Determine all legal considerations concerning the care and treatment of minor children (including unaccompanied minor children), such as consent, guardianship, decontamination consent, records privacy, and photographs of unidentified children.
- Appoint lawyers to serve as guardians ad litem for children orphaned or those who have lost a custodial parent.
- Include all relevant domestic courts (e.g., family, probate, juvenile) in the planning process to consider children's best interests.

Child Care: The Backbone of the Community

Audio Transcript

Recognizing the importance of child care for the community, Chevron contributed $500,000 to a nonprofit organization called Rebuild Jackson County, and provided work crews to repair and rebuild 40 child care centers in the county.

In Mississippi's other coastal counties, Chevron partnered with Save the Children, Help and Hope Foundation, the Mississippi Low Income Child Care Initiative, and U.S. Fund for UNICEF to repair, rebuild, and resupply 42 child care centers.

Mississippi State University's Early Childhood Institute also formed an initiative called Embrace Mississippi's Children and collected supplies, gifts, and cash contributions to resupply the centers.

To ensure that the rebuilt child care centers conformed to high standards, professional development training was required for each employee of the child care centers. In return, centers were resupplied with new playgrounds, educational materials, and developmental toys.

Thanks to the efforts of Chevron and numerous volunteer organizations, the centers could offer a higher quality of care than they had before the hurricane.

Lesson Summary

This completes this lesson. In this lesson you learned:

- The importance of various components of a community's infrastructure and facilities that support its children.
- Considerations when caring for children in disasters.

A disaster can disrupt these child support systems and negatively impact the physical and emotional well-being of a child. Therefore, in building an effective emergency operations plan, emergency managers should work with school officials, child care providers, and social services to ensure that these support systems are protected and can be brought back on line quickly and safely in the aftermath of a disaster.

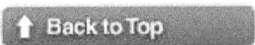

Lesson 4: Mitigation: Meeting Children's Needs During an Emergency

Lesson Overview

Reducing the impacts of future disasters is the goal of successful mitigation practices. The result is less disruption to the community and a quicker return to routine. Routine is very important to children for their physical and emotional well-being and for their education. Mitigation measures that reduce future disaster impacts on homes, schools, and child care facilities are critical to maintaining a child's everyday routine.

Upon completion of this lesson you should be able to:

1. Describe the steps of hazard mitigation planning process.
2. Explain how demographic and social conditions affect mitigation planning.
3. Explain mitigation best practices for schools and child care facilities.

A Close Call for Wichita Schools

Audio Transcript

On May 3rd, 1999, a series of deadly tornadoes swept through Oklahoma and Kansas. In the direct path of the storms were two schools in the Wichita Public School District.

According to the severe weather plan for these schools, in the event of a tornado, students were to take refuge in areas identified as the safe zones within the buildings: the hallways.

But when the tornadoes struck, these so-called safe zones were badly damaged. In one school, a tall boiler chimney collapsed into a hallway.

Luckily, the tornadoes passed through Wichita after school hours – this time. The storms were a wake-up call for the community. They realized how vulnerable the students were in the school buildings.

What if children were present the next time a tornado struck?

Sources:

- *Introduction to Emergency Management*. Second Edition. Haddow, George and Jane Bullock. Elsevier. Burlington, MA. 2006
- *Protecting School Children from Tornadoes: State of Kansas School Shelter Initiative.* FEMA Mitigation Case Studies, August 2002.

Hazard Mitigation Planning Process

Hazard mitigation planning is the process of determining how to reduce or eliminate the loss of life and property damage resulting from natural and human-caused hazards. The hazard mitigation planning process consists of the following steps:

- **Organize resources.**
- **Assess risks.**
- **Develop a mitigation plan.**
- **Implement the plan and monitor progress.**

Although the steps may be accomplished in order, hazard mitigation planning is rarely a linear process. For example, ideas developed while assessing risks may need revision, and additional information may need to be gathered while developing the mitigation plan. Additionally, implementing the plan may result in new goals or additional risk assessments.

Organize Resources

The first step of the mitigation planning process focuses on the resources needed. Steps performed when organizing resources include assessing your readiness to plan, establishing a planning team, securing political support, and engaging the community.

To successfully organize resources so the needs of children in disasters are met, you must ensure coordination among different agencies, integration with other planning efforts, and community involvement throughout the planning process. For example, when planning for the unique needs of children, you should coordinate with social services, medical professionals, schools, and child care facilities.

Assess Risks

Next, communities need to identify the characteristics and potential consequences of hazards. To accomplish this, the planning team will identify and evaluate natural hazards and prepare damage loss estimates.

When planning to meet the needs of children in disasters, it is important to understand how much of the community can be affected by specific hazards and what the impacts would be on the critical components of a child's world such as schools and child care facilities.

With this understanding, you can focus on your most important assets first to build the foundations of your mitigation strategy.

Develop a Mitigation Plan

Armed with an understanding of the risks posed by hazards, communities need to determine what their priorities should be. At this point, the planning team develops the mitigation goals and objectives and determines possible ways to avoid or minimize the undesired effects. The planning efforts are then captured in a written plan document. The result is a hazard mitigation plan and strategy for implementation.

Implement the Plan and Monitor Progress

The fourth step of the mitigation planning process involves adopting, implementing, monitoring, and reviewing the plan to ensure that the plan's goals and objectives are met. Communities can bring the plan to life in a variety of ways, ranging from implementing specific mitigation projects to changes in the day-to-day operation of the local government. Reviewing the plan periodically and making changes as needed will help keep the plan current, reflecting the changing needs of the community or state.

Mitigating Earthquake Damages

Imagine how you would feel if your children attended a school located along two of the most active faults in the country. That was the dilemma facing parents whose children attended the Castaic Union School District in southern California. After the 1994 Northridge Earthquake, the district conducted a risk assessment and learned that earthquake-related structural damage was not the only risk the district faced. The district's 63 buildings were also at risk for potential flooding from the nearby Castaic Dam, as well as fire or explosion from a rupture in oil pipelines that crossed the campus.

This information caused alarm about the safety of the district's facilities. If the dam failed or an oil pipeline broke during an earthquake, not only would the potential economic costs be enormous, but up to 1,200 students and 115 staff members would be at risk of injury or death.

Through a cost-benefit analysis, the district determined that the most feasible method to reduce their risks would be to condemn the structures on the old, high-risk site and relocate the campus to a low-risk area.

Through a combination of grant money from FEMA and the sale of bonds, the district relocated its facilities to an area that was completely out of the dam inundation area and far removed from the high-pressure oil pipelines. While the campus would still be within an active earthquake fault area, the new campus buildings would be constructed to fully conform to more current building code provisions, thus making them more resistant to seismic damage than the buildings being replaced.

Source: Haddow, G. & Bullock, J. (2006). *Introduction to Emergency Management* (2nd ed). Burlington, MA: Elsevier.

Mitigating Impacts on the Community

Every community should have a Community Hazard Mitigation Plan that identifies existing hazard risks in the community and proposes a strategy for mitigating these risks. Emergency managers should review their Community Hazard Mitigation Plan to determine how existing community risks may impact the critical infrastructure that directly or indirectly supports the needs of children. Community infrastructure to be examined includes:

- Community transportation network
- Public utilities
- Facilities
- Community transit system

The results of this review should be used to reconsider the priorities for mitigation projects currently included in the Mitigation Strategy in Community Hazard Mitigation Plan. Consideration should be given to designing and implementing mitigation measures that will reduce the impacts of future disasters on those elements of the community's critical infrastructure that directly or indirectly impact the children's infrastructure in the community.

Mitigating Ice Storm Damages

The ice storm of 2002 crippled the city of Independence, Missouri. Schools had to be closed. Thousands of residential customers were without power for several days - leaving many children without heat in their homes. One Salvation Army shelter even lost power. Storm damages exceeded $1.4 million.

With ice storms occurring in the area approximately every five years, reinstalling downed power lines every time ice toppled trees and snapped branches didn't make financial sense for Independence Power and Light (IPL). When a lineman was fatally electrocuted during repairs, it became clear that the cost was much too high. IPL knew that the only way to make a real difference would be to bury the power lines.

Mitigation funds became available after the storm was declared a Federal disaster, through the FEMA Hazard Mitigation Grant Program (HMGP). Teaming with Missouri's State Emergency Management Agency (SEMA), IPL sought mitigation grants to facilitate the underground conversion of service distribution lines to high-risk residential customers.

To date, IPL has buried more than 6,500 power lines from distribution line poles to residential structures, and has proven that this tactic saves money while enhancing power reliability, reducing property loss, and lessening risk to human life.

Mitigating Impacts on the Critical Components of a Child's World

Schools and child care facilities are the principal elements of the child infrastructure that supports children's everyday routines. Ensuring that these facilities will not only survive a disaster event but also remain functional is critical to maintaining the routine and education of the children in a community. Identifying the hazard risk relevant to each of these facilities in a community and designing and implementing hazard mitigation measures should be considered a priority in the community's overall hazard mitigation efforts.

Mitigating Hurricane Damages

Many long-time residents of Ocean Springs, Mississippi, vividly remember how Hurricane Camille's fury resulted in numerous deaths and widespread destruction in 1969, closing schools for weeks. Learning from experience, administrators of Ocean Springs Middle School vowed to develop techniques to reduce the loss of life and property in future disasters.

With partial funding from FEMA, the school installed permanent wind-resistant shutters on vulnerable classroom windows to help protect against strong winds charging in from the Gulf of Mexico.

When Hurricane Katrina made landfall on August 29, 2005, registering winds of up to 104 miles per hour, the shutters performed exceptionally well. They shielded windows from wind-borne objects and also protected the contents inside the building.

Without shutters, a window may be easily breached by hurricane winds. This creates tremendous upward pressure which may cause major roof failure, exposing the interior of the building to the storm.

After Hurricane Katrina, Ocean Springs Middle School remained intact and operational, unlike many public buildings in the city which were severely damaged and uninhabitable. In fact, the school served as a disaster command center immediately following the storm and later as a shelter for families who had lost their homes.

Mitigation Steps

The following are some general steps, recommended by the National Association of Child Care Resource and Referral Agencies (NACCRRA), that child care facilities, schools, and families can take to reduce the impact of different types of disasters:

- Regularly monitor for possible threats and hazards.
- Regularly clean and check heating, cooling, gas and electrical systems. Check that they are in good working order.
- Provide one or more carbon monoxide detectors, as well as regular maintenance and checks of smoke detectors.
- Ensure fire extinguishers are properly charged, mounted, and easy to reach in case of fire.
- Be sure key staff knows how to use a fire extinguisher properly and other staff or family members are trained in proper use.
- Ensure there are no barriers that prevent safe exit from the home or facility.
- Consider buying a generator for back-up power. A licensed electrician must install a generator.
- Inspect the facility for **potential hazards**.
- Work with your local first responders to learn more.

Potential Hazards

Potential hazards during a disaster include:

- Objects that could fall during an earthquake or tornado.
- Large items that could tip over during high winds, an earthquake, or similar event.
- Potential plumbing breaks during earthquakes and tornadoes.
- Materials that could easily ignite during a wildfire or other fire.
- Areas that will drain poorly during heavy rains and flooding.
- Windows or doors that are obstructed and from which adults and children could not evacuate during a fire or other disaster.
- Nearby rail lines that carry hazardous material.
- Hazmat manufacturing and storage facilities.

Agencies should be educated to think beyond the obvious. Zoning boards, real estate developers and council clerks can identify potential problems before the process is too far along.

Mitigating the Home

The destruction of a home can have a devastating impact on a child. Low- to moderate-income neighborhoods are often hardest hit by disasters. These homes may be located in a high risk area, such as in a floodplain or near industrial facilities that may release hazardous substances during a disaster. The type of construction found in these neighborhoods is also frequently substandard and unable to withstand high winds, flooding, and other effects of natural disasters.

Emergency managers must pay special attention to these areas and give them priority in implementing mitigation measures designed to protect children's homes. The Community Hazard Mitigation Plan identifies high risk residential neighborhoods in a community and provides recommendations on how to mitigate the risks in these areas.

Mitigation measures for flooding may include acquiring and relocating houses or elevating homes. For hurricanes, mitigation measures include installing storm shutters and hurricane clamps. For tornadoes, the most effective mitigation measure is to construct a safe room, an anchored and armored room that provides shelter from tornadoes even above ground. An example of a mitigation measure to guard against manmade disaster may be capping an abandoned landfill and installing extraction systems to prevent buildup of explosive landfill gases.

Hazard Mitigation Resources

FEMA provides funding for hazard mitigation projects through three major grant programs:

- The Hazard Mitigation Grant Program (HMGP) which makes funds available in the aftermath of a presidentially declared major disaster for mitigation projects. Any community in the State where the disaster declaration has been made with a certified Community Hazard Mitigation Plan is eligible for HMGP funding in the aftermath of a major disaster.
- The Flood Mitigation Assistance (FMA) Program was created as part of the National Flood Insurance Reform Act (NFIRA) of 1994 (42 U.S.C. 4101) with the goal of reducing or eliminating claims under the National Flood Insurance Program (NFIP). FEMA provides FMA funds to assist States and communities implement measures that reduce or eliminate the long-term risk of flood damage to buildings, manufactured homes, and other structures insurable under the NFIP.
- The Pre-Disaster Mitigation (PDM) Grant Program provides funds to states, territories, Indian tribal governments, communities, and universities for hazard mitigation planning and the implementation of mitigation projects prior to a disaster event. Funding these plans and projects reduces overall risks to the population and structures, while also reducing reliance on funding from actual disaster declarations. PDM grants are to be awarded on a competitive basis and without reference to state allocations, quotas, or other formula-based allocation of funds.

Communities should also consider creating a local funding source that could be used to match Federal, State and private sector funding for hazard mitigation projects. Two communities that have become models for disaster resilience are Tulsa, Oklahoma, and Napa, California. These communities have established consistent local funding sources that have helped pay for extensive hazard mitigation projects and programs.

Demographics

Understanding the demographic makeup of the community will help emergency managers in planning for a disaster. Using a **geographic information system (GIS)**, you can map your community to see where the households with children are located. You can also map schools, child care facilities, and other areas where children may gather.

You may also use another tool such as Google Maps to review the community centers such as house of worship, school, police and fire department stations in your area.

Geographic Information System (GIS)

A geographic information system (GIS) is a database system with software that can analyze and display data using digitized maps and tables for planning and decision-making. A GIS can assemble, store, manipulate, and display geographically referenced data, tying this data to points, lines, and areas on a map or in a table. GIS can be used to support decisions that require knowledge about the geographic distribution of people, hospitals, schools, fire stations, roads, weather events, the impact of hazards/disasters, etc. Any location with a known latitude and longitude or other geographic grid system can be a part of a GIS.

GIS is a very useful tool for many aspects of emergency management, including: emergency response, planning, exercises, mitigation, homeland security and national preparedness. In addition to its ability to manage and display data, GIS has robust modeling capabilities, allowing its users to adjust data and scenarios for prediction, planning and estimation.

The current trend in GIS is on web-based mapping. This capability can allow users to view an already created map or create maps, based on their own specifications, on their personal computers. Web-based mapping is expected to widely expand the use of GIS in the workplace, in schools, and in homes.

Source: Lauden, Kenneth C., and Lauden Jane P. 2000. Management Information Systems, 6th Edition, Prentice Hall Publishing Company: Upper Saddle River, NJ

Mitigating Flood Damages

During heavy rains, storm water often overflows the banks of the Mousam River in Kennebunk, Maine. Frequent flooding of homes in the Intervale neighborhood caused a ripple effect in the community, as pollution was carried downstream. Sewage, oil, gas, and asbestos washed up in families' yards and school playgrounds, putting area children at risk for disease and injury.

After much input from residents, the Town of Kennebunk decided that the only viable solution was to remove the willing homeowners from the floodplain either through buyouts or elevations. With the help of a FEMA Hazard Mitigation Grant Program (HMGP) grant, eight homes were elevated to protect them from the floods. The town acquired three other homes for demolition, and area fire departments burned the homes as a training exercise.

After these mitigation efforts, the Intervale neighborhood has reported no more flooding problems, as of February 2009.

A Close Call for Wichita Schools

Audio Transcript

As a result of the May 3rd event, during which two schools in the Wichita Public School District were damaged by tornadoes, a Presidential Disaster Declaration was made. The State of Kansas used funding from several Federal sources to identify and build additional protection measures for school children in the state.

In Wichita, 24 safe room projects were initiated within the public school district. Safe rooms provide above-ground protection from tornadoes.

The facilities will also protect many more community members who use the facilities for various activities such as precinct voting, church worship services, and community outreach and recreation.

In addition to building safe rooms, the community enhanced their processes for shelter management, including procedures for maintenance, inspections, and drills.

The emergency management agency in the county works closely with the schools to evaluate areas of refuge and make recommendations for the best methods to increase occupant safety.

The Wichita Public School District has set an example for implementing a school shelter initiative. Other Kansas school districts are following their lead to help ensure that, the next time disaster strikes, their children will be better protected.

Sources:

- Haddow, G. & Bullock, J. (2006). *Introduction to Emergency Management* (2nd ed). Burlington, MA: Elsevier.
- FEMA. (2002, August). *Protecting School Children from Tornadoes: State of Kansas School Shelter Initiative.* (FEMA Mitigation Case Studies). Available from FEMA's Resource and Document Library at http://www.fema.gov/media-library/assets/documents/3771.

Lesson Summary

This completes this lesson. In this lesson you learned:

- The steps in the hazard mitigation planning process.
- The effects of demographic and social conditions on hazard mitigation planning.
- Mitigation best practices for schools and child care facilities.

By being proactive, communities can protect their infrastructure from the effects of disasters. Remember, the hazard mitigation planning process consists of four basic steps which rarely occur in a linear progression:

- Organize resources.
- Assess risks.
- Develop a mitigation plan.
- Implement the plan and monitor progress.

You also learned about several best practices for protecting schools, child care facilities, and other critical components of a child's world. With these examples in mind, you should be able to better protect your community, and its children, by mitigating the effects of future disasters.

Lesson 5: Prevention

Lesson Overview

There are many actions a community can take to avoid an incident or to intervene to stop an incident from occurring. Prevention involves actions to protect lives and property. Child care facilities and schools must work closely with the community stakeholders, such as emergency managers, school officials, and emergency shelter managers to ensure that the needs of children are addressed in their emergency operations plans.

Upon completion of this lesson, you will be able to:

1. Define theimportance of prevention.
2. Identify prevention actions to increase the safety and security of a school or child care facility.
3. Identify opportunities for students' involvement in the safety of their school and the well-being of their school's community members.
4. Identify criteria for assessment of a school's or child care facility's level of involvement with law enforcement.
5. Identify prevention actions a school or child care facility may implement to prevent violence and promote mental health and well-being.

FEMA for Kids in Schools

Audio Transcript

The two steps you can take to protect your family be prepared for a disaster. One create a disaster supply kit. Two make a communications plan.

We let them know that FEMA is here to try to assist as possible as best we can. Then we tell them about preparing for a disaster, how to make a plan, a communication plan, as well as if they had someone in their family that has unique needs. We tell them the can build disaster kits, as well as a plan disaster supply kit. They really love that game. You want to play a game yea so let me hurry up and give you this great information.

We tell them what goes in the kit and why, and then we allow them to tell us if its yes or no. Extra batteries yes, water yes, the no would be my high heel boot and of course my pink shoe.

They love the disaster supply game, I think the kids are really responsive to it they really love it. If there is going to be a flood we need to evacuate quickly. We have to bring important things for all our family members, food water a weather radio.

The biggest advantage to sharing the information Is that you kind of allay some of their fears. I think they watch the news and they feel that they are helpless and when they know that there is concrete stuff they can take, and when they know that there are organizations there to provide support for their families and themselves, I think that kind of gives them some feeling of confidence and comfort so hopefully help them resist some of the panic should they be faced with some emergency.

FEMA does much more than just go out after an incident. They do emergency preparedness our children empowering children and families to address issues of emergency is so important.

This ends our presentation so give yourselves a hand.

Why Prevention

Schools and child care facilities are supposed to be safe havens, and have a duty to take care of their students. The reality is that most schools and child care facilities are very safe places – but for those unthinkable instances, schools need to take actions to respond.

An emergency operations plan provides a methodical way to think through the entire lifecycle of a potential crisis, helps determine required response and recovery capabilities and resource gaps, and helps stakeholders learn and practice their roles. Schools must plan for all emergencies they may face because:

- Schools and child care facilities have a legal and moral responsibility to protect students, faculty, and staff.
- For most emergencies, school and child care staff will be the initial responders.
- Effective prevention actions along with effective training and exercises can improve a school or child care facility's ability to protect, mitigate, respond to, and recover from emergencies.

Prevention Actions to Increase Facility Security and Maintain a Safe Environment

All schools and child care facilities work to prevent violence. Remind students, staff, and parents of their important role in promoting safety by following procedures and reporting unusual or concerning individuals or behavior. It also may be helpful to address the important balance between sufficient building security and providing students a healthy, nurturing, normal environment by starting with a maintenance and security safety checklist.

Maintenance and Security Safety Checklist

Use the following checklist to assess the school's current level of safety related to the development of your EOP. If an element is in place, check YES. If changes need to be made, check IMPROVE. If the element is not in place, check NO. If the school plans to implement this missing element, check IMPLEMENT. In some cases, an element may be not applicable (N/A) to your school. Although this checklist is more appropriate for schools it can also be modified for child care facilities.

Checklist Element	Yes	No	N/A	Implement	Improve
1. All exterior doors have non-removable hinge pins.					
2. Exterior doors, unless designated for entry, have no exterior hardware.					
3. Exterior doors have a protective plate covering locks.					
4. Double doors have an astragal					
5. All operable windows have hardware in working condition.					
6. Required exit doors are equipped with panic hardware.					
7. Hallways leading to required exit doors are kept clear and unencumbered with furniture.					
8. A master key control system is in place to monitor keys and duplicates.					
9. Doors accessing internal courtyards are tied into the central alarm system.					
10. The school has developed written regulations regarding access to and use of the building by school personnel after regular school hours.					
11. Staff members who remain after hours are required to sign out.					

12. Staff members must lock unoccupied classrooms when not in use.					
13. High-risk areas such as the office, cafeteria, computer rooms, music room, shops and labs are protected by high security locks and an alarm system.					
14. The security alarm system receives regular maintenance and/or testing.					
15. Building security at night is provided by either: • adequate exterior directional lighting, or • total blackout.					
16. All school equipment is permanently marked with an identification number.					
17. The school maintains record of all maintenance on doors, windows, lockers, and other areas of the school.					
18. One person is designated to perform the following security checks at the end of each day: • Check that all classrooms and offices are locked. • Check all restrooms and locker rooms to ensure that everyone has left the building. • Check all exterior entrances to ensure that they are locked. • Check all night-lights to ensure that they have been turned on. • Check the security alarm system.					
19. The school has a maintenance schedule for checking:					

• Lights • Locks and other hardware • Storage sheds/areas • Portable classrooms (trailers) • Other					

This checklist was adapted from Virginia Department of Education. (2000). School Safety Audit Protocol. Available from http://www.doe.virginia.gov/support/safety_crisis_management/school_safety/audits/sch_safety_audit_protocol.pdf

Student Involvement in the Safety and Security of their School

Schools are recommended to provide opportunities for students to be represented on the school planning or exercise team. Other methods to include students can include highlighting violence prevention programs and curriculum currently being taught in school. Emphasize the efforts of the school to teach students alternatives to violence including peaceful conflict resolution and positive interpersonal relationship skills. Cite specific examples such as Second Step Violence Prevention, bully proofing, or other positive interventions and behavioral supports. A checklist of prevention actions that can be taken to increase students' involvement in prevention may also be created to assess the school's current level of safety related to opportunities for student involvement.

Involving Students in Prevention Checklist

Use the following checklist to assess the school's current level of safety related to opportunities for student involvement. If an element is in place, check YES. If changes need to be made, check IMPROVE. If the element is not in place, check NO. If the school plans to implement this missing element, check IMPLEMENT. In some cases, an element may be not applicable (N/A) to your school. Although this checklist is more appropriate for schools it can also be modified for child care facilities.

Checklist Element	Yes	No	N/A	Implement	Improve
1. Students are represented on the school planning and/or exercise team.					
2. The school provides opportunities for student leadership related to prevention and safety issues.					
3. The school provides adequate recognition opportunities for all students.					
4. Students are provided encouragement and support in establishing clubs and programs focused on safety.					
5. Students are adequately instructed in their responsibility to avoid becoming victims of violence, (i.e., by avoiding high-risk					

situations and seeking help from adults).					
6. Students have the opportunity to participate in a conflict resolution program.					
7. Students have the opportunity to learn about bullying prevention, as well as conflict resolution, the prevention of sexual harassment, and prevention of suicide.					
8. The school provides some form of an anonymous hot line whereby students may report incidents or suspicious activities.					

This checklist was adapted from Virginia Department of Education. (2000). School Safety Audit Protocol. Available from
http://www.doe.virginia.gov/support/safety_crisis_management/school_safety/audits/sch_safety_audit_protocol.pdf

Partnerships with Law Enforcement

Schools and child care facilities need to consider partnering closely with career law enforcement officers, to collaborate with to prevent incidents. These plans may include (A) educate students in crime and illegal drug use prevention and safety; (B) develop or expand community justice initiatives for students; and (C) train students in conflict resolution, restorative justice, and crime and illegal drug use awareness. Schools may review the Partnering with Law Enforcement Checklist to assess the school's current level of involvement with law enforcement. Although this checklist is more appropriate for schools it can also be modified for child care facilities.

Partnering with Law Enforcement Checklist

Use the following checklist to assess the school's current level of involvement with law enforcement. If an element is in place, check YES. If changes need to be made, check IMPROVE. If the element is not in place, check NO. If the school plans to implement this missing element, check IMPLEMENT. In some cases, an element may be not applicable (N/A) to your school. Although this checklist is more appropriate for schools it can also be modified for child care facilities.

Checklist Element	Yes	No	N/A	Implement	Improve
1. The school reports incidents of crime and violence to law enforcement officials.					
2. Law enforcement personnel are an integral part of the school's safety planning process.					
3. The school has developed and maintained an effective relationship with law enforcement.					

4. The school and local law enforcement have developed a memorandum of agreement, (MOA), defining the roles and responsibilities of both.					
5. Law enforcement personnel provide a visible and regular presence on campus during school hours and at school-related events.					
6. Law enforcement provides after hours patrols of the school site.					

This checklist was adapted from Virginia Department of Education. (2000). School Safety Audit Protocol. Available from
http://www.doe.virginia.gov/support/safety_crisis_management/school_safety/audits/sch_safety_audit_protocol.pdf

Preventing Violence and Supporting Mental Health and Well-Being

Administrators can reinforce the importance of safety by creating a caring community in which adults and students respect and trust each other and children feel connected, understand expectations, and receive the behavioral and mental health support they need. Schools and child care facilities may want to review whether students have access to conflict resolution programs or have assistance in developing anger management skills. Other prevention and intervention areas include bilingual and multicultural resources as well as the prevention of harassment needs to be emphasized school wide. For a detailed checklist to assess the school's current level of safety related to mental health and well-being, click on the highlight words.

School Violence Prevention and Intervention Checklist

Use the following checklist to assess the school's current level of safety related to prevention and intervention efforts. If an element is in place, check YES. If changes need to be made, check IMPROVE. If the element is not in place, check NO. Although this checklist is more appropriate for schools it can also be modified for child care facilities.

Checklist Element	Yes	No	N/A	Implement	Improve
1. Students have access to conflict resolution programs.					
2. Students are assisted in developing anger management skills.					
3. Prevention of harassment is emphasized school wide.					
4. Bilingual and multicultural resources are available to students and staff members.					

5. Programs are available for students who are academically at-risk.					
6. Students may ask for help without the loss of confidentiality.					
7. Students and parents are aware of community resources.					
8. A bully prevention program is in place.					
9. The school has a well developed network of service providers to which students can be referred.					
10. Crisis prevention is an integral part of the school's safety plan; that is, practice of emergency drills and evacuation, a partnership with law enforcement officials, metal detection capability, and adequate adult monitoring at all times.					
11. Adequate suicide prevention support systems are in place for students.					
12. The school has implemented a character education program in accordance with the State code.					

This checklist was adapted from Virginia Department of Education. (2000). School Safety Audit Protocol. Available from
http://www.doe.virginia.gov/support/safety_crisis_management/school_safety/audits/sch_safety_audit_protocol.pdf

Lesson Summary

This completes this lesson. In this lesson you learned:

- The importance of prevention
- Prevention actions to increase the safety and security of a school or child care facility.
- Opportunities for students' involvement in the safety of their school and the well-being of their school's community members.
- Criteria for assessment of a school's or child care facility's level of involvement with law enforcement.
- Prevention actions a school or child care facility may implement to prevent violence and support mental health and well-being.

Prevention involves actions to protect lives and property. Child care facilities and schools must work closely with the community stakeholders, such as emergency managers, school officials, and emergency shelter managers to ensure that the needs of children are addressed in their emergency operation plans.

 Back to Top

Lesson 6: Response

Lesson Overview

Recent disasters starting with Hurricane Katrina have brought the unique needs of children in disasters to the attention of emergency planners, medical officials, social service agencies, and voluntary groups involved in disaster response and recovery. The lessons learned and the knowledge gained from these recent events should inform the work to be done to better prepare for and respond to the needs of children in future disasters.

Upon completion of this lesson, you will be able to:

- Identify staff roles for evacuation/relocation, shelter-in-place, and lockdown.
- Identify procedures that should be addressed by a school's or child care facility's emergency operations plan.
- Describe the services needed by children in shelters and the agencies that provide them.

A Narrow Escape

Audio Transcript

As Valerie drove her children home from school on April 9th, 2009, she kept a watchful eye on the smoke filling the sky near her neighborhood. Throughout the day, she had heard reports of wildfires sweeping across the state of Oklahoma, and now it appeared the danger was approaching her home.

With her husband, Matt, on deployment to the Middle East, Valerie felt nervous dealing with this crisis alone, but she was a Navy wife who knew how to be strong.

When they arrived home, Valerie told her children, nine-year-old Jake and six-year-old Natalie, that there was a fire nearby and they may have to leave again soon.

She turned on the television to watch for reports of the fire's location, while the children unloaded their backpacks to show her the papers they had done in school.

Jake chatted about the classmates who had received his birthday party invitations and said they could come to his sleepover in a few weeks.

From the living room windows, Valerie could see smoke billowing high into the air. Then suddenly, she saw a volunteer firefighter rushing across her yard to grab the water hose from the patio. She stepped out to ask what she should do, and the firefighter told her to turn on her sprinkler system.

What they had no way of knowing at that moment was how quickly the fire would spread. Wind gusts of over 60 miles per hour were launching the flames through the air and making them impossible to control.

Valerie went into the garage to turn on the sprinklers, but she had operated the system only once and couldn't get it to come on. Little Natalie followed her, barefoot, with the family puppy tagging along behind. Valerie grabbed the puppy and told Natalie to get her shoes back on.

Then suddenly, the firefighter was yelling that the neighbor's yard was on fire, and they needed to leave.

With only a few seconds to get out of the house, Valerie had just enough time to grab her purse and get her children and the puppy to the car. By the time the family made it out of the driveway, their entire front yard was engulfed in flames.

The EOP in Action

When a disaster occurs, emergency managers must put the Emergency Operations Plan (EOP) into action by mobilizing response teams and notifying key agencies. Among the agencies that must be notified are schools and child care providers. Emergency managers should develop and maintain a list of schools and child care providers in their community that should be notified of potential and/or pending disaster events. Contact your local first responders for notification options.

The Agency for Healthcare Research and Quality, in its 2009 study entitled *School-Based Emergency Preparedness: A National Analysis and Recommended Protocol,* provided guidance to school officials for how to use this notification information that would lead to evacuation/relocation, sheltering-in-place, or lockdown.

Recommended Roles for School Personnel During Evacuation/Relocation, Shelter-in-place, or Lockdown

Role	Evacuation / Relocation	Shelter-in-place	Lockdown
Principal	Make an announcement over the PA system while crisis team members deliver instructions to key staff.	Make an announcement over the PA system and mobilize the crisis team. Designate staff who would take responsibility for "sweeping" the hallways and bathrooms to ensure that children are in the proper places and are accounted for.	Initiate lockdown if a threatening, suspicious, or violent intruder is found in the building; trying to enter the building; or if their imminent presence is suspected. Dial 911 and notify town emergency responders. Make an announcement over the PA system. Mobilize the crisis team.
Crisis Team	Initiate the response. Inspect the building and direct students to exits and assembly areas. Carry walkie-talkies and cell phones. Communicate with town emergency response teams. Communicate regularly with staff regarding the status of the emergency.	Inspect the building and playground and direct staff and students to shelter area. Communicate with town emergency responders. Maintain communication with the central office (or other incident command center) using walkie-talkies or cell phones.	Attempt to identify the area of intrusion. Maintain communication using walkie-talkies or cell phones.
Secretarial Staff	Bring the attendance roster for students and staff to the alternate site, and take the go kit.	Bring the attendance roster for students and staff and the substitute list.	Dial 911 and contact the principal if they witness a violent situation. Bring the attendance roster for students and staff and the substitute list. Bring the go kit to a safe location in the building.
Teachers and Other Support Staff	Assist children with mobility difficulties. Take their classroom go kit. Lead students through evacuation using designated routes. Check lavatories and other areas of the building where students may be unsupervised in order to assure evacuation is complete. Take attendance and report any missing	Move students indoors to the common area. Assist children with mobility difficulties. Take attendance and inform the crisis team of any children that are missing. Close all windows and doors, and pull down shades prior to exiting the classroom. Place a wet paper towel over the nose and mouth for temporary respiratory protection, inform the	Contact the central office immediately if they witness a violent or potentially violent situation. Have students in the hallway enter their classroom. Check lavatories and have those students using the facilities enter the closest classroom. Turn off lights, lock classroom doors and windows, and, if it is safe to do so, pull the shades.

	students to a crisis team member. Lead their students to the off-site location in the event of relocation following the designated route. Stay with their students until further instructions are given.	incident command center and, potentially, relocate to another part of the building if there appears to be contamination within the shelter. Remain with their students until an "all clear" is given.	Keep students away from windows and doors. Take attendance and report missing and extra students to the office. Have students stop and drop to the floor if a gunshot or explosion is heard. Maintain a calm environment and reassure students that everything is being done to return the situation to normal. Remain in the classroom until further instructions are given by the principal.
School Nurse	Bring the emergency medical kit and the first aid kit. Bring student emergency cards and medical information. Monitor students with special medical needs and notify the administration of any urgent medical needs.	Follow instructions for school staff if students are in the health room. Bring the emergency medical kit and the first aid kit. Bring student emergency cards and medical information. Monitor students with special medical needs, and notify the administration of any urgent medical needs.	Dial 911 and contact the principal if they witness a violent situation. Follow instructions for lockdown if students are in the health room, and communicate with other members of the crisis team.
Custodians	Maintain communication with the administration who may assign specific tasks. Inspect the building following an evacuation. Assume responsibility for building safety and carry a school floor plan, which includes the location of utility shut-off valves.	Shut down the classroom/building HVAC system. Turn off local fans in the area. Close doors and windows.	Lock all entrances to the building. Maintain communication with administration. Carry school floor plan showing shut-off valves for all utilities.

Source: Agency for Healthcare Research and Quality. (2009, January). *School-Based Emergency Preparedness: A National Analysis and Recommended Protocol.* (Pub No. 09-0013). Rockville, MD: Author.

Preserving Family Unity when Evacuating

A sudden onset disaster event such as an earthquake may require that schools and child care facilities in a community evacuate and relocate students and children to a new location. Emergency managers must work with local school officials and child care providers to ensure that plans are in place as to how such an evacuation would proceed, how parents will be notified about the location to which children will be evacuated.

Preserving family unity is the most important step you can take to provide for the physical safety and emotional stability of children in disasters. Without sufficient planning, children can become separated from their families and other caregivers. Because family separation can occur even when well-prepared evacuation plans are carried out, it is also important to identify protocols for reuniting families as quickly as possible.

Inadequate Strategies for the Evacuation of Children with Their Parents, Families, or Caretakers

During and after Hurricane Katrina, scores of children were found wandering alone in search of lost adults. Some children later described swimming past bloated human and animal corpses and lacerating their legs on unseen objects in the water below in efforts to find their parents. Some parents reported that during the evacuation, they placed their children on earlier buses in the mistaken belief that when the adults got seats on a later bus, the whole family would end up in the same place. In some cases, the children who were found were too young to give their names or too traumatized to speak, even if they were of age to talk. In other cases, investigators had no photographs of the children to circulate because the pictures were left behind in the floods. In the Houston Astrodome, a center was set up where volunteers worked to reunite children with their parents. Digital photographs were taken of each child. The photos and any information obtained were placed in the database of the National Center for Missing and Exploited Children. The volunteers also had a very long list of children who had been reported missing by a parent.

Source: Dolan, M. & Krug, S. (2006). "Pediatric Disaster Preparedness in the Wake of Katrina: Lessons to Be Learned." In *Clinical Pediatric Emergency Medicine*. Atlanta, GA: Elsevier.

Evacuation of Child Care Facilities and Schools

The National Association of Child Care Resource and Referral Agencies (NACCRRA) recommends that child care programs must have an evacuation plan in place that addresses the questions listed below. These questions are also applicable to schools, clubs, after-school programs, and other groups that provide services for children:

- Who can direct an evacuation?
- How will the parents be notified?
- What will the children be told?
- What signal will be given to notify everyone in the facility?
- How will all staff, children, volunteers, and others in the facility be accounted for?
- What medications, supplies, and records will be taken during evacuation?
- To where will children, staff, and others be evacuated?
- How will children and staff be transported?
- What coordinating actions with community public safety and/or emergency management officials are necessary?
- How will the utilities be shut off?
- Who is responsible for each action?

Evacuation Kits for Child Care Programs

Every child care facility should have evacuation kits containing the following:

- First-aid kits
- Critical medications for staff and children
- Emergency contact information for each child:
  - Parents' work phone
  - Parents' cell phone
  - Parents' home phone
  - Parents' home and work e-mail addresses
  - Two emergency contacts in area (preferably individuals who don't live or work with parents)
  - Two emergency contacts out of area
  - Phone number and e-mail of parents' supervisors
  - Critical medical information
  - Permission to transport and seek medical treatment
- Emergency contact information on staff
  - Spouse or family member's work phone
  - Staff member's cell phone
  - Spouse or family member's cell phone
  - Home phone
  - Staff member's home e-mail address
  - Spouse or family members' work e-mail address
  - Two emergency contacts in area
  - Two emergency contacts out of area

- Critical medical information
- Dry or canned infant formula
- Appropriately-sized diapers (with enough for an extended period, if necessary)
- Sufficient supply of potable water
- Disposable cups
- Baby food and plastic spoons
- Food bars in individual wrappers
- Games, books, and other materials to keep children occupied

Source: National Association of Child Care Resource and Referral Agencies (NACCRRA). (2006). *Is Child Care Ready? A Disaster Planning Guide for Child Care Resource and Referral Agencies*.

Responding to Children's Needs in Shelters

When a disaster strikes and people are evacuated to shelters, it is important to consider not only their physical needs, such as a roof over their heads and a place to sleep, but also their mental and emotional needs. Children are especially vulnerable during times of upheaval and require special attention and care in shelters.

Historically, the American Red Cross has been responsible for setting up and managing emergency shelters in the immediate aftermath of a disaster event. The American Red Cross has relied on other voluntary agencies such as the Church of the Brethren, the Southern Baptists Convention, and the Salvation Army to provide child care services to families living in shelters. After Hurricane Katrina, the American Red Cross, Children's Disaster Services, and Save the Children signed a Memorandum of Understanding (MOU) to facilitate quick establishment of Child-Friendly Spaces in shelters run by the American Red Cross.

Incorporating Safe Spaces into the Emergency Operations Plan

By planning ahead, you can ensure that the needs of children are met when they must be evacuated. In New York City, for example, Save the Children and the city's Office of Emergency Management (OEM) signed an agreement to incorporate Save the Children's Safe Spaces program into New York City's emergency sheltering plan so the city can set up play areas in evacuation shelters and other places.

Under the initiative, Save the Children will provide 1,075 Safe Space Kits for use in emergency shelters in New York City.

As part of the plan, more than 1,000 volunteers will be trained to lead activities for children in shelters. The kits will be stored in OEM's shelter stockpile, along with other supplies that can be quickly deployed to as many as 509 pre-identified shelter locations.

The kits contain:

- Materials to mark off a special area for children.
- Activity supplies such as art materials, books, blocks, scarves and balls.
- Materials to help schedule activities, check children in and out, and sanitize toys.

Children's Disaster Services: Meeting the Needs of Children

Children's Disaster Services (CDS), of the Church of the Brethren, strives to meet the needs of children by setting up child care centers in shelters and disaster assistance centers across the nation. Specially trained to respond to traumatized children, volunteers provide a calm, safe, and reassuring presence in the midst of the chaos created by tornados, floods, hurricanes, wildfires, and other disasters.

Volunteers from across the country undergo a rigorous screening process and participate in specialized experiential training in which they learn to work with children after a disaster. The volunteers are capable of mobilizing rapidly and responding both locally and nationally. When volunteers arrive at a disaster location, they are equipped with a "Kit of Comfort" containing carefully selected toys that promote imaginative play. Volunteers give children individualized attention and encourage them to express themselves, thereby starting the healing process. Although many volunteers are motivated by faith, CDS' training is open to anyone over 18 years old.

In addition to the volunteers who respond to disasters, CDS maintains a special **Critical Response Child Care (CRC) team** to work with the children when a mass casualty event occurs.

Critical Response Child Care Team

The Critical Response Child Care (CRC) team is a group of experienced Children's Disaster Services volunteers who have received additional training that prepares them to work with children after a mass casualty event such as an aviation incident. The presence of a compassionate care giver, along with carefully selected play activities, has a significant impact on the recovery of a child who has experienced the trauma of such a loss.

A six-member team is on call each month, ready to travel within four hours of deployment by the American Red Cross. When the volunteers arrive, they work in a Family Assistance Center, where those impacted by the incident participate in briefings and receive support from the American Red Cross. This partnership between the American Red Cross, Children's Disaster Services, and Save the Children ensures that children's needs are being met in an appropriate and compassionate manner.

Inadequate Preparations for Mental Health Interventions for Children

Thousands of children were among the 25,000 people crowded into the New Orleans Superdome and the New Orleans Convention Center for protection from Katrina and the subsequent flooding. Evacuees within these centers reported excessive heat, crowding, acts of violence, poor sanitation, inadequate fluids and food, and the overt presence of medically ill and dead persons. For many reasons, including interagency delays and confusion, relief personnel were unable to access these evacuees with basic essentials, including mental health services. Evacuation from these centers did not begin for two days after the hurricane was over. Mental health services, including play therapy and art therapy for the children, did not begin until well after the evacuations and certainly did not include all of the affected children or all shelters. In one instance, women residing in the neighborhood near one of these shelters were the ones to provide crayons and paper for the evacuated children so that these children could begin to express the experiences they had been through.

Source: Dolan, M. & Krug, S. (2006). "Pediatric Disaster Preparedness in the Wake of Katrina: Lessons to Be Learned." In *Clinical Pediatric Emergency Medicine*. Atlanta, GA: Elsevier.

Children's Disaster Services: Supporting Families and Communities

CDS provides respite, education, and individualized consultation for parents about their child's unique emotional needs after a disaster. When picking up their children, parents often start to talk with CDS volunteers. Parents share concerns and worries with the volunteers who have cared for their children for the past few hours. The volunteers, who have been trained in what is typical behavior for children after a disaster, can reassure parents about the child's adjustment, give parents printed resources about helping traumatized child, or refer parents to appropriate community resources.

Children's Disaster Services will also provide workshops and/or consultation to community agencies, schools, and other organizations about their unique needs relative to disaster, trauma, and children.

Other Disaster Response Organizations

When disaster strikes, volunteer organizations are quick to arrive and lend a helping hand. Voluntary Organizations Active in Disaster (VOAD) members provide vital services including food, shelter, clothing, and counseling during disaster response efforts. The contributions of these organizations are invaluable, and although not all VOAD members can be highlighted in this course, two groups that are often active during response are the Salvation Army and the Southern Baptist Convention (SBC) Disaster Relief.

The Salvation Army is often among the first on the scene when disaster strikes. The primary aim of the Salvation Army in disaster relief is to meet the basic needs of those who have been affected, both survivors and first responders. Their goals are to offer material, physical, emotional, and spiritual comfort. The Salvation Army delivers meals and drinks to disaster victims and emergency workers, provides emergency shelter, supports cleanup and restoration efforts, manages donations of goods, and provides spiritual and emotional care during times of crisis. The Salvation Army Team Emergency Radio Network (SATERN) also helps provide emergency communications when more traditional networks, such as telephones, are not operating.

SBC Disaster Relief is a partnership ministry of the state Baptist conventions and the North American Mission Board, Southern Baptist Convention. SBC has approximately 2,000 mobile units and more than 88,000 trained volunteers who provide a variety of services during and after disasters, such as providing hot meals, child care, and showers, as well as doing laundry, making repairs, and removing debris.

Responding to Legal Issues

The American Bar Association (ABA) Center on Children and the Law, partnering with the National Council of Juvenile and Family Court Judges (NCJFCJ) and the National Center for State Courts, aids legal and judicial system responses to the needs of children and families affected by disasters.

Their responses in the past have centered around three areas of assistance:

- Determining and helping meet the more immediate needs of dependency courts and child welfare legal offices in disaster-affected areas.
- Helping serve the legal needs of affected children and families through provision of pro bono child welfare law experts.

- Studying child welfare legal issues affecting children and families in disasters, including needed state and federal legislative responses.

For more information, view the ABA's website http://www.americanbar.org.

Responding to Medical Issues

When a crisis occurs and children with special health care needs must access the emergency system, they are often left vulnerable because of a lack of access to information about their medical problems. There can be delays in treatment, unnecessary tests, and sometimes serious errors as a result of lack of access to information available to the treating emergency physician.

To help ensure prompt and appropriate care for children with special healthcare needs, the American Academy of Pediatrics (AAP) and the American College of Emergency Physicians (ACEP) created the Emergency Information Form (EIF). Although the EIF is increasingly being used by primary care providers, subspecialists, and emergency departments (EDs), it has not been widely disseminated to EMS agencies. As part of your community's disaster planning efforts, this form should be distributed to EMS agencies. During response, it can be used to transfer critical information about children with special health needs. For children registered with the program, the MedicAlert® Foundation serves as a repository for the data collected via the EIF.

Children with Special Healthcare Needs

During and after Hurricane Katrina, children with special healthcare needs, particularly the subset of technology-dependent children, experienced increased morbidity and mortality because of inadequate planning to provide for backup electricity to run essential life-sustaining equipment, such as suction, ventilators, and nebulizers. Local emergency medical services (EMS) agencies were generally unaware of the technology-dependent children in their areas who needed immediate evacuation to centers with electricity and medical personnel; therefore, they were unable to provide such assistance. The press related accounts of children with special healthcare needs being evacuated in private vehicles on interstate highways with essential equipment, such as respirators, running out of battery power.

Source: Dolan, M. & Krug, S. (2006). "Pediatric Disaster Preparedness in the Wake of Katrina: Lessons to Be Learned." In *Clinical Pediatric Emergency Medicine*. Atlanta, GA: Elsevier.

Emergency Medical Services for Children

The Federal Emergency Medical Services for Children (EMSC) Program is designed to ensure that children and adolescents, no matter where they live, attend school, or travel, receive appropriate care in a pre-hospital health emergency. It is administered by the U.S. Department of Health and Human Services' Health Resources and Services Administration's Maternal and Child Health Bureau. Since its establishment, the EMSC Program has provided grant funding to all 50 states, the District of Columbia, and five U.S. territories.

The Federal EMSC Program supports two resource centers.

EMSC National Resource Center

The National Resource Center (NRC), located just outside Washington, DC, was established in 1991 to help improve the pediatric emergency care infrastructure throughout all 50 states, the District of Columbia, and the five U.S. territories. The NRC is housed within Children's National Medical Center, one of America's leading pediatric institutions serving sick and injured children and their families. The NRC works with states to identify the resources needed to organize and implement EMSC activities throughout the nation. By using the NRC, communities can learn from each other's experiences and adopt proven models.

National EMSC Data Analysis Resource Center

The National EMSC Data Analysis Resource Center (NEDARC) assists EMSC grantees and state EMS offices in developing their own capabilities to collect, analyze, and utilize EMS and other healthcare data to improve the quality of care in state EMS and trauma systems. NEDARC is part of the University of Utah in Salt Lake City, UT.

Emergency Response Communications

Within a disaster zone, the traditional methods of communication may no longer work. For example, in the days after Hurricane Katrina, broadband internet, land-line telephones, and cell phones all failed. Emergency responders, schools, child care facilities, and others charged with the safety of children, should have back-up communications in place such as:

- Runners
- Hand-painted signs

- Posters and fliers
- Radio and television stations
- Amateur radio
- Walkie-talkies
- Satellite telephones

Source: Needle, S. (ca 2005). *A disaster preparedness plan for pediatricians*. Elk Grove Village, IL: American Academy of Pediatrics. Available from https://www.aap.org/en-us/advocacy-and-policy/aap-health-initiatives/children-and-disasters/documents/disasterprepplanforpeds.pdf

A Narrow Escape

Audio Transcript

After Valerie and her children narrowly escaped the wildfires threatening their home, they found a friend to stay with for the night. Jake asked what they were going to do about the sleepover he had planned for his tenth birthday. Valerie didn't know what to tell him.

She called a neighbor and learned that a camera crew was broadcasting from in front of her house at that moment. The neighbor told her which channel to turn to and warned her that the news was not good. Valerie changed the channel and saw her house, completely engulfed in flames.

She watched in shock as her home burned to the ground, with nothing more than bricks left standing. Then she had to tell Jake and Natalie that their home was gone, and with it, all their toys and clothes. Jake's sleepover would have to be cancelled, but she assured him they would still have a party to celebrate his birthday.

Although she was concerned about how her children would cope with losing everything, Valerie knew the family would be all right. Insurance would replace the material things they lost, and most importantly, they still had each other.

Thanks to a volunteer firefighter, her children were safe, and that's all that mattered.

Lesson Summary

This completes this lesson. In this lesson you learned:

- Staff roles for evacuation/relocation, shelter-in-place, and lockdown.
- Procedures that should be addressed by a school or child care facility's emergency operations plan.
- Services needed by children in shelters and the agencies that provide them.

The lessons learned and the actions prescribed by such groups as the American Academy of Pediatrics, the National Association of Child Resource and Referral Agencies (NACCRRA) and others have outlined the steps that emergency managers and stakeholders responsible for children need to take to ensure that the unique needs of children are addressed in all phases of the response to a disaster event.

Lesson 7: Recovery

Lesson Overview

Because stable routines are vital to the physical and emotional well-being of a child, restoring the critical components of a child's world quickly in the aftermath of a disaster is essential. Children and families will also need help dealing with the emotional impact of the disaster and the losses they have experienced as a result.

Upon completion of this lesson, you will be able to:

- Explain the three main priorities for helping children to return to their normal routine and education.
- Discuss the factors that lead to resilience among children faced with disaster.

AFT Teachers Discuss Rebuilding

Audio Transcript

Well a monster tornado was bearing down on Birmingham this is debris it's not very often that we actually see this … this is a monster tornado.

What we have never seen before in this part of Alabama for tornadoes that were miles wide and were just unrelenting, one right after the other. The rumbling, the ears popping, that awful moaning and groaning sound. Some people say it sounded like a freight train.

Here is She-ey town, here's Bessemer and this tornado …

I was watching TV and it said She-ey town but it didn't mention by the road. I got up and walked to the hall which is the center of my house. And I could see the cloud coming. I thought I've got to get somewhere. The wind just knocked me down flat on my back. A wall and a chest of drawers landed on me. But then evidently I lost consciousness.

The next thing I knew somebody was calling my name. It was a cousin. I kept saying I'm in the bedroom not knowing that my house was gone. My husband passed away four years ago. And I don't know if I'm comin but apparently it was not my time. It took about 15 men to get the debris off of me. They put me on a door, put me on a four-wheeler and took me about ½ a mile to the shopping center. From there they stabilized me.

That night, all of us, our Birmingham, AFT, our Jefferson AFT, we were trying to contact members. The calls about to make sure she was okay. I got in touch with Crystal but I couldn't get in touch with Victoria. And that's when we found out Pleasant Grove was hit.

A lot of the neighbors were out, checking on each other. It was very scary, very scary time. We lost some neighbors and some good friends as well in the storm. We've just been offering our support to their families. It's going to take a while for them to I guess bounce back from this. And my superintendent called and told me we had lost one of our members. And gave me the contact information. And this member lived in the Pleasant Grove area. She was a friend to everybody. She was just a wonderful person. As small as she was her heart was so big. She rarely ever had any bad works to say to people or disagreements with people. She was just that type of person.

The next thing I decided once I heard some of the devastation I wanted to go out myself to see how bad it was. I actually rode every place in Jefferson County in Birmingham to see what was going on and that was McDonald Chapel popped up. It is a suburb right outside of Birmingham so it is in a wooded area. And what I did was I went in and found out where it was hidden. I immediately picked up the phone because I knew nobody had been up there. And I called the office and told them they had to get to the McDonald Chapel and bring everything we had because they people hadn't got anything. They thanked us and still thanking us today. You know that's what you're supposed to do at a time like that.

We were able to get past this so that we can get behind the lines to assist people. So we saw some incredible sights and some things I hope we never get to see again. And I remember there was this one little old lady in Concord and the only thing left was a closet in her house and she refused to leave. So for several days our staff took food and water and things that she needed. The fourth day the agency really started getting to some of these communities but we were able to get to them from the very beginning.

Well the AFT , ever since the tornado hit we have been out there, everywhere – Concord, Pleasant Grove, Blunt County, Colman County. And we've had a lot of our members just volunteering. That's what we do. We get out there and help. There's a lot of kids just don't have anything. There's clothes here, shoes here. There's toys here. Anything these people use and we are going to get it to them.

We knew the student population was hit very hard. But I would never thought when I did my numbers in Birmingham, I had a high school that had 1300 students and 500 students were homeless. And I had an elementary school South Hampton really just tore my heart when I found the school had 408 students and 300 of the students were homeless. We made a vow that we would make sure both school districts started the school back so that the kids would have some sense of something normal. When you lost everything, you know the least you can do is open up the school doors so that they can have a meal for that time.

If we have a summer program I'm going to work this summer with the children. I'll be right there. I'm on schedule. See what they did with my arms? I'm bandaged in April. That's where my heart is. I miss them.

One of the greatest things that we're trying to find a ways to plug the people into counseling and care …

I'm proud of AFT. I'm proud of our members. They have done everything they can to help and I am so proud of our community, our churches, all the groups we work with. It's been a community effort and that's what it's all about and take for the long term to help all the children and all the employees who have been impacted.

You can still go back to Pleasant Grove and like a bomb hit. What it reminds me of is going through a dump with paved road through it.

It's all gone.   My whole block is gone. All my neighbors are gone you know. But we plan to eventually build back. I'm coming back home where I was.

Seventy-five percent of Pleasant Grove has been devastated but I believe Pleasant Grove will rebound and we will build back better. So that is my fervent hope.

Heavenly Father we thank you for this day, for this opportunity that we've been given to remember and honor Tracy Traeweek, a very special person to those of us gathered here this memorial service on her behalf.

I am really honored here today as we dedicate this tree in front of this Board of Education in the honor of Tracy.

The plaque that AFT has provided us is lovely. You said it's all good. We know God made Tracy good and Tracy was happy to live life just the way it was.

That's the only thing I could ask if they could just remember the good things and how she brought so much joy to our family knowing their life is what it is because of Tracy.

Priorities for the Restoration of a Child's World

There are three main priorities for helping children return to their normal routine and education:

- Provision of temporary housing, schools, and child care facilities where needed.
- Restoration of the child infrastructure in place in the community prior to the disaster.
- Provision of mental health services for children and caregivers as they recover from the disaster.

Each of these priorities will be discussed in detail throughout this lesson.

Provision of Temporary Housing

When families are displaced, it is important for them to have a safe and healthy place to go. Without proper planning, families can end up in dangerous conditions such as homes that are unhealthy to live in or overcrowded neighborhoods where crime becomes a problem.

After Hurricane Katrina, one family of seven lived for many months in an 8 by 30 foot travel trailer in an interim housing facility near Baton Rouge. The family had to sleep in shifts, and the family's six-year-old boy, Hakeem, feared he would be sent to a foster home.

Hakeem's Fears

At only six years old, Hakeem has learned to hide his fears and sadness behind a brave smile. He is a bright, active child who plays video games and conducts imaginary battles between an array of superhero action figures. Sitting close to his grandmother, Valerie, in a cramped unit of the Renaissance Village trailer park, he proudly says his ABCs and then counts to 110. But he displays his fears with frequent nosebleeds and bedwetting.

Hakeem lives in the small trailer with his grandparents, aunt, and three other children. Hakeem's mother, Angel, is not there. Valerie had to tell him that he would not see his mother again. When Hurricane Katrina hit, Angel was unable to handle the impact of the tragedy. She severed relations with her family and abandoned Hakeem. When the family contacted her by telephone, she changed her number to an unlisted one. Hakeem knows other children in foster care and he's always watching for signs his grandmother might give him away. Valerie is constantly reassuring the child that she won't do that. "We always have to watch our body language," she said.

Valerie, who has suffered from seizures brought on by stress, must look after her own mental health while holding the rest of her family together. Her husband had a stroke and is delusional. The family depends on the free food provided by the Renaissance Village cafeteria because they make too much money to get food stamps. The family's income is $1,200 a month from Julius's retirement, of which $700 goes to pay the mortgage on their home in New Orleans that was a total loss.

They are in a Catch-22. If they default on their mortgage, they lose their claim to a recent flood insurance settlement. Valerie doesn't expect a payout for five to seven months. Until then, the family can't move into a stable home. Valerie's car has broken down and she feels stuck.

Hakeem's emotional health depends on Valerie who is struggling to cope herself. Speaking of what she and her family have been through, Valerie said, "I wouldn't wish this on my worst enemy, and I have none. I'm all cried out."

Sources:

- Children's Defense Fund (2006). *Katrina's Children: A Call to Conscience and Action.* Available from http://www.childrensdefense.org/library/data/katrinas-children-call-conscience-action-hurricane-2006.pdf
- Children's Defense Fund. (2007). *Katrina's Children: Still Waiting.* Available from http://www.childrensdefense.org/library/data/katrinas-children-still-waiting-hurricane-2007.pdf

Provision of Temporary Schools and Child Care Facilities

Minimizing interruption to a child's education and reducing disruption to social support systems are critical factors in a child's recovery from a disaster. Providing educational services and child care also allows parents to return to work after a disaster. Without these essential services, a community's recovery from disaster stagnates. Communities need to plan for how to provide temporary educational and child care services for children affected by disaster – whether the children are from the local community or another.

When emergency management officials assess risks to the facilities in the community as part of the planning process, they should consider not only which schools and child care facilities may be vulnerable to damage, but which facilities in less vulnerable areas may be able to provide temporary services to displaced children.

Emergency managers should work with schools and child care facilities in their community to ensure that Emergency Operations Plans are in place and that the facilities have determined ways to handle an overflow of students resulting from damage to other facilities in the community or a disaster elsewhere.

At times, an event may cause damage that is beyond the scope of the disaster planning efforts. It's important for emergency management officials and others tasked with the care of children to be flexible and creative in order to provide for the needs of children during and after a disaster.

Emergency Child Care in Mississippi Gets Parents Back to Work

When Hurricane Katrina struck Pass Christian, Mississippi, virtually all of the homes, buildings, and businesses were damaged or destroyed. Five months later, nearly all of Pass Christian's 7,000 residents still lived in temporary travel trailers on what was left of their property. Another 200 people lived in a FEMA tent camp called "The Village."

For the community to begin recovery, people needed to return to work – which meant that quality child care was a critical need. Unfortunately, the child care centers had all been destroyed.

To help parents return to work, a tented child care center was established in The Village – the first of its kind to be constructed in an emergency setting in the U.S. The child care center was the result of Save the Children's partnership with the city of Pass Christian, the Mississippi Department of Health's child care licensure office, and Ginger Holmes, the owner of the Pass Christian Child Development Center. In addition, educational materials, an outdoor play structure, and child care supplies were donated from the *Bright Horizons Foundation* and *Bridging the Gulf*. The site, located in four tents in the center of the town, served more than 40 children daily - from infancy through pre-school age.

The emergency child care tents in Pass Christian provided an innovative solution which could be used as a model to be replicated in other crisis situations throughout the United States.

Source: Save the Children (ca 2005). *Emergency Child Care in Mississippi Gets Parents Back to Work.* [Press Release]. Fairfield, CT: Save the Children Federation, Inc.

Restoration of the Existing Child Infrastructure

While temporary housing, schools, and child care facilities are important for disaster recovery, restoring these critical components of a child's world to what they were before the disaster will help rebuild a sense of stability for children and families.

Communities may be able to work with charitable organizations and volunteers to help restore child care services. For example, Save the Children played a leadership role in a child care recovery coalition that repaired and re-supplied 39 child care facilities in seven Mississippi counties affected by Hurricanes Katrina and Rita.

Plaquemines Parish

Plaquemines Parish, Louisiana, was almost completely washed away by flood waters from Hurricane Katrina. During the recovery period, many residents lived in temporary housing such as in Diamond Park, an interim housing facility that originally held 450 trailers.

To cultivate a protective environment for children living in temporary housing, Save the Children sponsored the Safe and Protective Communities Project. The project's goals were to help bring residents together, establish spaces where the community members could congregate, and create safer environments for children. Save the Children also worked with the Plaquemines Parish Government, KaBOOM!, and Project Rebuild Plaquemines to construct a new universally accessible playground in Diamond Park.

Using a trailer donated by YMCA, a community center was established, where children can play games in a computer lab, watch movies on a big screen television, and create arts and crafts projects. The facility was also used for programs run by organizations like YMCA, Save the Children, Emergency Communities, and the Boys and Girls Club.

In addition, professional photographers used the center to conduct a photography workshop called the 450 Photo Experience, teaching children to express themselves through photography.

The playground, community center, and photography workshop have been instrumental in helping the children in Plaquemines Parish make sense of their world as they recover from the devastation of Hurricane Katrina.

Planning for Children to Return Home

Communities should plan for ways to help residents transition from temporary housing to permanent homes. After Hurricanes Katrina and Rita, FEMA provided displaced homeowners with trailers and federal funds to repair or rebuild their homes. However, many residents faced unemployment due to the closure of businesses and industries in the area, which caused economic hardships and made rebuilding difficult or impossible. As of April, 2009, more than 5,000 Gulf Coast families were still living in temporary housing.

Organizations in your area, such as a local **Habitat for Humanity** affiliate, may be able to help rebuild homes in the community, thus helping residents transition to permanent housing.

Habitat for Humanity

Through volunteer labor and donations of money and materials, Habitat for Humanity builds and rehabilitates simple, decent houses which are sold to partner families at no profit and financed with affordable loans.

Habitat is not a giveaway program. Homeowners are required to make a down payment and monthly mortgage payments, and this money is then used to help build more homes. Homeowners also invest hundreds of hours of their own labor, referred to as "sweat equity," to build the Habitat house as well as the houses of others.

Every Habitat affiliate follows a nondiscriminatory policy of family selection, and homeowners are selected based on their level of need, their willingness to become partners in the program, and their ability to repay the loan.

You can find out more about Habitat for Humanity at their website, http://www.habitat.org.

The Perils of Living in an Abandoned Neighborhood

Many New Orleans families who rented their homes before Hurricane Katrina were unable to return to the city because of skyrocketing prices. After living in Houston for a year, Cheryl and her two daughters were able to return to New Orleans because their former landlord repaired a four-plex in the upper Ninth ward and rented it to them at a reasonable price. But theirs was one of only three inhabited houses in the entire block. Cheryl worried about her children living in a largely abandoned neighborhood. She had heard about rats inhabiting homes left untouched since the storm, homeless people roaming the streets, and rampant crime. When her children returned home from school at the end of the day, they didn't go out again, because it wasn't safe.

Children's Defense Fund. (2007). Katrina's Children: Still Waiting. Available from http://www.childrensdefense.org/library/data/katrinas-children-still-waiting-hurricane-2007.pdf

Mental Health Services

Parents and other caregivers can take steps to help children deal with the effects of a disaster and to better cope with the next disaster. Children can develop confidence by knowing what events may impact their lives and how they can be part of the way their family deals with those events. Local mental health programs should be designed prior to the event to help children cope with the emotional effects of disaster. Psychosocial programs are an example of national programs that are available from a variety of resources such as Save the Children.

Save the Children's Journey of Hope programs incorporate movement, art, music, and literacy, and are tailored to children of different age groups as well as caregivers to provide an opportunity for discussing issues such as anger, sadness, and self-esteem. Save the Children also offers Resilient and Ready workshops, designed to educate children and build resilience when faced with various forms of disasters.

Save the Children trains social workers, mental health providers, and school- and community-based personnel to lead these programs.

Comfort for Kids

After the attacks of September 11, 2001, Mercy Corps partnered with Bright Horizons Family Solutions, JPMorgan Chase, and the Dougy Center for Grieving Children and Families to support children affected by the disaster. They assembled Comfort Kits, stocked with stuffed animals and age-appropriate materials explaining what happened, for thousands of children in and around New York City. The group also provided training to parents and adult professionals, including 150 special-victims detectives from the NYPD, about how to deal with affected children.

In 2005, when Hurricanes Katrina and Rita struck, Comfort for Kids was reactivated, and 50,000 Comfort Kits were distributed in several cities to which children had been evacuated. In addition, Mercy Corps developed age-appropriate workbooks designed to help children make sense of their individual hurricane experiences. The organization also provided training for caregivers in Louisiana, Mississippi, and Texas, using a booklet and accompanying facilitator's guide called "What Happened to MY World?"

Factors for Building Resilience

Several factors are important to building resilience.

- Connectedness, commitment, and shared values
- Participation
- Structure, roles, and responsibilities
- Support and nurturance
- Critical reflection and skill building
- Resources
- Communication

These elements are interrelated. For example, families are more likely to participate in community activities when they feel connected to the community. In a disaster, this may translate into increased willingness to follow urgent community directives such as when to evacuate or where to shelter in place. Through connectedness and participation, families gain an understanding of community structure and the roles and responsibilities they have before, during, and after a disaster.

Community support of families and children further increases their resilience. After communities respond to disasters and resources are expended, leaders can critically reflect and assess how effective was the response, and they can make improvements before another event.

Essential to all the elements is communication. Only with clear, consistent communication will information be heard, utilized, and lead to productive change for managing future situations and enhanced resilience.

Source: Gurwitch, R. H., Pfefferbaum, B., Montgomery, J. M., Klomp, R. W., & Reissman, D. B. (2007). *Building community resilience for children and families*. Oklahoma City: Terrorism and Disaster Center at the University of Oklahoma Health Sciences Center.

Helping Children Cope with Disaster

In a disaster, children look to adults for help. They learn how to react to an emergency by observing how the adults in their lives react. The responses of parents and other caregivers during and after a disaster may have a lasting impact on the emotional stability of children.

After a disaster, children are most afraid that the event will happen again, someone will be injured or killed, they will be separated from the family, or they will be left alone. Parents can help their children cope with these fears by addressing the factors for building resilience.

FEMA and the American Red Cross have developed a resource called "Helping Children Cope with Disaster" that provides information and advice for parents to guide them through the recovery process with their children.

Factors for Building Resilience	Ways that Parents Can Help Children Cope
Connectedness, commitment, and shared values	<ul><li>Keep the family together as much as possible.</li><li>Allow children to return to normal activities as soon as possible, to connect them with their peers and caregivers.</li><li>Encourage children to volunteer and help others.</li></ul>
Participation	

	• Include children in recovery activities. • Include children in discussions and planning. • Provide opportunities for children to participate in school, cultural, faith-based, or extracurricular activities.
Structure, roles, and responsibilities	• Assign chores and responsibilities to children. • Educate children about their roles during a disaster. • Provide consistency in their routines.
Support and nurturance	• Reassure children with firmness and love. • Be patient and understanding, and give children extra time and attention. • Hug children often and hold them when they need comforted. • Provide opportunities for children to interact with extended family, other caregivers, and their peers.
Critical reflection and skill building	• Encourage children to describe what they're feeling and allow them to speak freely about what scares or puzzles them. • Provide creative play opportunities.
Resources	• Watch for changes in your children's behavior, and seek help from a mental health specialist or clergy member if the child does not respond to the other suggestions.
Communication	• Calmly and firmly explain the situation, including what will happen next. • Use positive behavior and language around children. • Encourage children to ask questions and listen when they talk. • Try to answer questions and address concerns with concrete, easy-to-follow information. • Give constructive information about how they can be prepared to protect themselves. • Limit exposure to the media (e.g., television, radios, computers, and reporters who want to interview the children).

Sources: Adapted from

American Red Cross. (2004). *Helping Children Cope with Disaster* Jessup, MD: Federal Emergency Management Agency. Available from http://www.redcross.org/images/MEDIA_CustomProductCatalog/m14740413_Helping_children_cope_with_disaster_-_English.pdf

Gurwitch, R. H., Pfefferbaum, B., Montgomery, J. M., Klomp, R. W., & Reissman, D. B. (2007). *Building community resilience for children and families*. Oklahoma City, OK: Terrorism and Disaster Center at the University of Oklahoma Health Sciences Center.

Save the Children. (2014). *How to help children cope with disasters: 10 tips from Save the Children* ("Get Ready. Get Safe." campaign). Available from http://www.savethechildren.org/atf/cf/%7B9def2ebe-10ae-432c-9bd0-df91d2eba74a%7D/GRGS_10_TIPS_FOR_COPING.PDF

The Importance of Play

Play time is essential for children. Playing allows children to express their emotions, provides an outlet for their energy, and helps relieve tension. Therefore, providing opportunities for children to play in a safe environment is crucial to their recovery from disaster.

The following strategies are recommended by the National Association for the Education of Young Children for helping children deal with trauma:

• Give worried children more time for relaxing, therapeutic experiences such as playing with sand, water, clay, and play dough.
• Provide plenty of time and opportunities for children to work out their concerns and feelings through dramatic play. In dramatic play, children can pretend that they are big and strong to gain control over their trauma and to overcome feelings of helplessness.
• Spend more time outdoors, at the gym, or in the park so children have opportunities for physical activity that provides an emotional release.

Sharing Stories to Heal

Audio Transcript

Kim Carr of RaiseSomeHope.org speaking:

RaiseSomeHope.org. We are hope raisers and we go about the healing after the tornado. The children from the neighborhood and the school behind that building demolished are coming and getting their free shirts. They color beautifully. Sometimes they start with black and as they share their stories and are with their friends teachers come when they share it with each other it starts the process of healing.

Kim Carr continuing:

We were able to get a whole truckload of bricks. They colored them beautifully. They date it and so they all have a little piece of their school.

Kimberly Martinez, Plaza Towers Elementary School teacher:

I only had about ten that were still here once the tornado hit. Several parents had pulled their children out. And luckily we were able to get all of them either into the girls or boys bathrooms and it saved our lives that day.

Erin Ogdon, Plaza Towers Elementary School teacher:

I helped out with the Pre K children and we all covered them while they were curled up in a ball. And while we covered them a wall fell on us. Most of my kids, they were able to wiggle their way out.

Terry Whatley, Retired Moore School teacher:

I was with a FEMA representative surveying what was left and they told me to come around the corner and I loved the message that was on her shirt, so I came to get one. My heart goes out to those who have lost lives and those children. Comfort and strength in their families.

Lesson Summary

This completes this lesson. In this lesson you learned:

- Three main priorities for helping children to return to their normal routine and education.
- Factors that lead to resilience among children faced with disaster.

The factors that lead to resilience and should be addressed when helping children cope with disaster are:

- Connectedness, commitment, and shared values
- Participation
- Structure, roles, and responsibilities
- Support and nurturance
- Critical reflection and skill building
- Resources
- Communication

There are numerous programs designed to help children, parents, and caregivers to cope with the impacts of a disaster. Community-based and non-profit groups should partner with local emergency managers to ensure these programs are delivered in schools, summer camps, after school programs and in child care facilities.

Lesson 8: Course Summary

Lesson Overview

This lesson provides a brief summary of Planning for the Needs of Children in Disasters course.

Course Summary

This course provided you with information and resources to aid you in revising an emergency operations plan for your community or organization so you can effectively plan for the unique needs of children in disasters.

The Unique Needs of Children in Disasters

In Lesson 2, you learned:

- Types of threats to the physical security of children in disasters.
- The emotional impact a disaster may have on a child.
- The critical role of the family to children in a disaster.

When developing the emergency operations plan, your community or organization must consider ways to protect children from physical harm and ensure that appropriate medical care is available for children injured in disasters. Your plan should also address methods for enhancing children's emotional stability because it can be easily disrupted by a disaster event. Programs are available to help children and caregivers plan for disasters and cope with them after an event occurs.

Family unity is critical to children's physical security and emotional stability. Steps must be taken before a disaster to reduce the chances that families will be separated and ensure that, if they are separated, the families are reunited in a timely and careful manner.

Exploical Components of a Child's World

In Lesson 3, you learned:

- The importance of various components of a community's infrastructure and facilities that support its children.
- Considerations when caring for children in disasters.

A disaster can disrupt these child support systems and negatively impact the physical and emotional well-being of a child. Therefore, in building an effective emergency operations plan, emergency managers should work with school officials, child care providers, and social services to ensure that these support systems are protected and can be brought back on line quickly and safely in the aftermath of a disaster.

Mitigation: Meeting Children's Needs During an Emergency

In Lesson 4, you learned:

- The steps in the hazard mitigation planning process.
- The effects of demographic and social conditions on hazard mitigation planning.
- Mitigation best practices for schools and child care facilities.

By being proactive, communities can protect their infrastructure from the effects of disasters. Remember, the hazard mitigation planning process consists of four basic steps, which rarely occur in a linear progression:

- Organize resources.
- Assess risks.
- Develop a mitigation plan.
- Implement the plan and monitor progress.

You also learned about several best practices for protecting schools, child care facilities, and other critical components of a child's world. With these examples in mind, you should be able to better protect your community, and its children, by mitigating the effects of future disasters.

Prevention

In Lesson 5, you learned:

- The importance of prevention
- Prevention actions to increase the safety and security of a school or child care facility.
- Opportunities for students' involvement in the safety of their school and the well-being of their school's community members.
- Criteria for assessment of a school's or child care facility's level of involvement with law enforcement.
- Prevention actions a school or child care facility may implement to prevent violence and support mental health and well-being.

Prevention involves actions to protect lives and property. Child care facilities and schools must work closely with the community stakeholders, such as emergency managers, school officials, and emergency shelter managers to ensure that the needs of children are addressed in their emergency operations plans.

Response

In Lesson 6, you learned:

- Staff roles for evacuation/relocation, shelter-in-place, and lockdown.
- Procedures that should be addressed by a school's or child care facility's emergency operations plan.
- Services needed by children in shelters and the agencies that provide them.

The lessons learned and the actions prescribed by such groups as the American Academy of Pediatrics, the National Association of Child Resource and Referral Agencies (NACCRRA) and others have outlined the steps that emergency managers and stakeholders responsible for children need to take to ensure that the unique needs of children are addressed in all phases of the response to a disaster event.

Recovery

In Lesson 7, you learned:

- Three main priorities for helping children to return to their normal routine and education.
- Factors that lead to resilience among children faced with disaster.

The factors that lead to resilience and should be addressed when helping children cope with disaster are:

- Connectedness, commitment, and shared values
- Participation
- Structure, roles, and responsibilities
- Support and nurturance
- Critical reflection and skill building
- Resources
- Communication

There are numerous programs designed to help children, parents, and caregivers to cope with the impacts of a disaster. Community-based and non-profit groups should partner with local emergency managers to ensure these programs are delivered in schools, summer camps, after school programs and in child care facilities.

Tookit

A Toolkit is available for you to download that contains valuable resources to aid you as you work to revise the emergency operations plan for your community or organization You can find this toolkit under the Resources Button in the top right hand corner of each screen of the course. The Toolkit also contains a list of the individuals, agencies, and organizations that contributed to the development of the course, as well as references used in this course.

This Toolkit is a downloadable document in portable document format (PDF).

To download a PDF file, you must have Adobe Acrobat Reader software installed on your system.

Conclusion

This concludes the Planning for the Needs of Children in Disasters course.

The purpose of this course is to provide you with the tools and confidence to become more effective in planning and meeting the unique needs that arise among children as a result of a disaster or emergency.

You now have the resources and knowledge to revise an emergency operations plan for your community or organization to effectively address the unique needs of children in disasters.

The course exam follows.

Congratulations and good luck!

FEMA | Planning for the Needs of Children in Disasters
TOOL KIT

FEDERAL EMERGENCY MANAGEMENT AGENCY
EMERGENCY MANAGEMENT INSTITUTE

Planning for the Needs of Children in Disasters

Toolkit:
Resources and Acknowledgements

FEDERAL EMERGENCY MANAGEMENT AGENCY
EMERGENCY MANAGEMENT INSTITUTE

IS 366

Table of Contents

NOTE:

FEMA EMI has provided this list of resources to provide information that may be of interest to emergency managers, implementers of children's programs, and others involved in planning for the needs of children in disasters.

EMI does not guarantee that outside websites and non-government documents listed in this Toolkit comply with the requirements of Section 508 (Accessibility Requirements) of the Rehabilitation Act.

This Toolkit may contain URLs that were valid when originally published, but now link to sites or pages that no longer exist.

Resources for Emergency Management Officials

While not an all-inclusive list, the following websites and documents will help emergency management officials when planning for the unique needs of children in disasters.

Web Links

- American Red Cross Disaster Preparation Training
  http://www.redcross.org/services/prepare/0,1082,0_239_,00.html

- Church World Service Emergency Response Program, Disaster Recovery Help
  http://www.disasterrecoveryhelp.org

- Council of State Archivists: Intergovernmental Preparedness for Essential Records Project
  http://www.statearchivists.org/iper/index.htm

- The Homeland Security Exercise and Evaluation Program (HSEEP) Volumes
  https://hseep.dhs.gov/

- International Association of Emergency Managers
  http://www.iaem.com/

- Special Population Planner
  http://sourceforge.net/projects/spc-pop-planner/

- Tips for Managing and Preventing Stress: A Guide for Emergency and Disaster Response Workers (943 KB)
  http://mentalhealth.samhsa.gov/cmhs/Katrina/workers.asp

- FEMA Resources:

  - Flood Mitigation Assistance Program
    http://www.fema.gov/government/grant/fma/fma2009.shtm

  - Hazard Mitigation Grant Program
    http://www.fema.gov/government/grant/hmgp/index.shtm

  - Interactive Web-based course: Basics of Individual Assistance
    http://training.fema.gov/ocean/IS403/IA_Menu.htm

  - Mapping and Analysis Center
    http://www.gismaps.fema.gov/gis01.shtm

  - Mitigation Planning
    http://www.fema.gov/plan/mitplanning

  - Pre-Disaster Mitigation Grant Program
    http://www.fema.gov/government/grant/pdm/index.shtm

- Models for Disaster Resilience:

  - Napa, California, Flood Control & Water Conservation
    http://www.countyofnapa.org/Pages/DepartmentContent.aspx?id=4294968277

  - Tulsa, Oklahoma, Stormwater Management Plan
    http://www.cityoftulsa.org/CityServices/FloodControl/StormwaterPlan.asp

Downloadable Documents

- Building Community Resilience for Children and Families (2,101 KB)
  http://www.nctsnet.org/nctsn_assets/pdfs/edu_materials/BuildingCommunity_FINAL_02-12-07.pdf

- FEMA Publications Catalog (284 KB)
  http://www.fema.gov/doc/library/femapubcatalog.rtf

- Help in Child Welfare Legal and Judicial System Responses to Children and Families Affected by Disasters (48 KB)
  www.abanet.org/child/disasters.pdf

- Mitigation Planning How-to Guide, "Getting Started: Building Support for Mitigation Planning" (1,824 KB)
  Available from: http://www.fema.gov/library/viewRecord.do?id=1867

- The Unique Needs of Children in Emergencies: A Guide for the Inclusion of Children in Emergency Operations Plans (320 KB)
  www.savethechildren.org/publications/emergencies/Children-in-Emergencies-Planning-Guide.pdf

Resources for School Administrators and Teachers

While not an all-inclusive list, the following websites and documents will help school administrators and teachers when planning for the unique needs of children in disasters. Also see the Resources for Children page.

Web Links

- American Academy of Pediatrics: Children & Disasters
  http://www.aap.org/disasters/schools.cfm

- American Red Cross Disaster Preparation Training
  http://www.redcross.org/services/prepare/0,1082,0_239_,00.html

- American Red Cross Masters of Disaster® Educator's Kit
  http://www.redcross.org/preparedness/educatorsmodule/ed-cd-main-menu-1.html

- Church World Service Emergency Response Program, Disaster Recovery Help
  http://www.disasterrecoveryhelp.org

- Community Arise Training Curriculum
  http://www.cwserp.org/ (Click Resources, then Community Arise)

- Council of State Archivists: Intergovernmental Preparedness for Essential Records Project
  http://www.statearchivists.org/iper/index.htm

- Emergency Preparedness for Teachers, Students, and Families
  http://readyclassroom.discoveryeducation.com/

- God's Can Do Kids and Renew U Curriculum
  http://www.ldr.org/care/children.html

- National Association of School Psychologists: Helping Children After a Natural Disaster: Information for Parents and Teachers
  http://www.nasponline.org/resources/crisis_safety/naturaldisaster_ho.aspx

- National Association of School Psychologists: School Safety and Crisis Resources
  http://www.nasponline.org/resources/crisis_safety/index.aspx

- National Center for School Crisis and Bereavement
  http://www.cincinnatichildrens.org/svc/alpha/s/school-crisis/default.htm

- National Clearinghouse for Educational Facilities
  http://www.edfacilities.org/

- Pandemic Influenza Tabletop Exercise Materials, Minnesota Department of Health
  http://www.health.state.mn.us/divs/idepc/diseases/flu/pandemic/scexercise/index.html

- Readiness and Emergency Management for Schools Technical Assistance Center
  http://rems.ed.gov/index.cfm?event=resources

- Tips for Talking About Disasters
  http://mentalhealth.samhsa.gov/cmhs/EmergencyServices/after.asp

- U.S. Department of Education
  http://www.ed.gov

- FEMA Resources:

- EMI School Program
  http://training.fema.gov/emiweb/emischool/

- Interactive Web-based course: Basics of Individual Assistance
  http://training.fema.gov/ocean/IS403/IA_Menu.htm

- Interactive Web-based Course: IS-362 Multi-Hazard Emergency Planning for Schools
  http://www.training.fema.gov/EMIWeb/IS/is362.asp

- Resources for Parents and Teachers
  http://www.fema.gov/kids/teacher.htm

Downloadable Documents

- American Red Cross Masters of Disaster® Quick Start Guide for Educators (467 KB)
  http://www.redcross.org/www-files/Documents/pdf/education/quickstartguide.pdf

- Building Community Resilience for Children and Families (2,101 KB)
  http://www.nctsnet.org/nctsn_assets/pdfs/edu_materials/BuildingCommunity_FINAL_02-12-07.pdf

- Coping with Disasters: A Guidebook to Psychosocial Intervention (252 KB)
  www.mhwwb.org/CopingWithDisaster.pdf

- FEMA Publications Catalog (284 KB)
  http://www.fema.gov/doc/library/femapubcatalog.rtf

- The Importance of Play in Promoting Healthy Child Development and Maintaining Strong Parent-Child Bonds (281 KB)
  www.aap.org/pressroom/playFINAL.pdf

- Listen, Protect, and Connect: Psychological First Aid for Children, Parents, and Other Caregivers After Natural Disasters (184 KB)
  Available from: http://www.cincinnatichildrens.org/svc/alpha/s/school-crisis/psych-aid.htm

- Practical Information on Crisis Planning: A Guide for Schools and Communities (1,662 KB)
  www.ed.gov/emergencyplan/crisisplanning.pdf

- Resilience for Kids and Teens: A Guide for Parents and Teachers (385 KB)
  Available from: http://www.apahelpcenter.org/featuredtopics/feature.php?id=39

- School-Based Emergency Preparedness: A National Analysis and Recommended Protocol (189 KB)
  Available from: http://www.ahrq.gov/prep/schoolprep/

- STEP: Student Tools for Emergency Planning Information Sheet (84 KB)
  www.nedrix.com/presentation/0309/STEP%20One%20Page.pdf

- What Happened to MY World? Helping Children Cope with Natural Disaster and Catastrophe Participant Manual (970 KB)
  Available from: http://www.mercycorps.org/publications/11846

- What Happened to MY World? Helping Children Cope with Natural Disaster and Catastrophe Facilitator's Guide (2,077 KB)
  Available from: http://www.mercycorps.org/publications/11857

Resources for Child Care Providers

While not an all-inclusive list, the following websites and documents will help child care providers when planning for the unique needs of children in disasters. Also see the Resources for Children page.

Web Links

- American Academy of Pediatrics: Children & Disasters
  http://www.aap.org/disasters/child-care.cfm

- American Red Cross Disaster Preparation Training
  http://www.redcross.org/services/prepare/0,1082,0_239_,00.html

- Church World Service Emergency Response Program, Disaster Recovery Help
  http://www.disasterrecoveryhelp.org

- Community Arise Training Curriculum
  http://www.cwserp.org/ (Click Resources, then Community Arise)

- Council of State Archivists: Intergovernmental Preparedness for Essential Records Project
  http://www.statearchivists.org/iper/index.htm

- Emergency Preparedness for Teachers, Students, and Families
  http://readyclassroom.discoveryeducation.com/

- God's Can Do Kids and Renew U Curriculum
  http://www.ldr.org/care/children.html

- The Institute for Business & Home Safety
  http://www.disastersafety.org/

- Model for Child Care Readiness: Tulsa Partners
  http://tulsapartners.org

- National Association of Child Care Resource & Referral Agencies, Children and Disasters
  http://www.naccrra.org/disaster/

- FEMA Resources:

  - Ready Business
    http://www.ready.gov/business

  - Ready Business (Spanish)
    http://www.listo.gov/negocios

  - Independent Study Course: IS-394.a Protecting Your Home or Small Business From Disaster
    http://training.fema.gov/EMIWeb/IS/IS394A.asp

  - Resources for Parents and Teachers
    http://www.fema.gov/kids/teacher.htm

Downloadable Documents

- Building Community Resilience for Children and Families (2,101 KB)
  http://www.nctsnet.org/nctsn_assets/pdfs/edu_materials/BuildingCommunity_FINAL_02-12-07.pdf

- Coping with Disasters: A Guidebook to Psychosocial Intervention (252 KB)
  www.mhwwb.org/CopingWithDisaster.pdf

- FEMA Publications Catalog (284 KB)
  http://www.fema.gov/doc/library/femapubcatalog.rtf

- The Importance of Play in Promoting Healthy Child Development and Maintaining Strong Parent-Child Bonds (281 KB)
  www.aap.org/pressroom/playFINAL.pdf

- Is Child Care Ready? A Disaster Planning Guide for Child Care Resource & Referral Agencies (15,418 KB)
  http://www.naccrra.org/disaster/docs/Disaster_Guide_MECH.pdf

- Listen, Protect, and Connect: Psychological First Aid for Children, Parents, and Other Caregivers After Natural Disasters (184 KB)
  Available from: http://www.cincinnatichildrens.org/svc/alpha/s/school-crisis/psych-aid.htm

- Resilience for Kids and Teens: A Guide for Parents and Teachers (385 KB)
  Available from: http://www.apahelpcenter.org/featuredtopics/feature.php?id=39

- What Happened to MY World? Helping Children Cope with Natural Disaster and Catastrophe Participant Manual (970 KB)
  Available from: http://www.mercycorps.org/publications/11846

- What Happened to MY World? Helping Children Cope with Natural Disaster and Catastrophe Facilitator's Guide (2,077 KB)
  Available from: http://www.mercycorps.org/publications/11857

Resources for Medical Professionals

While not an all-inclusive list, the following websites and documents will help medical professionals when planning for the unique needs of children in disasters.

Web Links

- American Academy of Pediatrics: Children & Disasters
  http://www.aap.org/disasters/pediatricians.cfm

- Center for Disaster Medicine: Pediatric Preparedness
  http://www.pediatricpreparedness.org

- Children's Health Fund
  http://www.childrenshealthfund.org

- Council of State Archivists: Intergovernmental Preparedness for Essential Records Project
  http://www.statearchivists.org/iper/index.htm

- Emergency Medical Services for Children
  http://bolivia.hrsa.gov/emsc/

- EMSC National Resource Center
  http://www.childrensnational.org/EMSC/

- National Emergency Medical Services for Children Data Analysis Resource Center
  http://www.nedarc.org/nedarc/index.html

Downloadable Documents

- A Disaster Preparedness Plan for Pediatricians (623 KB)
  www.aap.org/disasters/pdf/disasterprepplanforpeds.pdf

- Emergency Information Form (83 KB)
  http://www.aap.org/advocacy/blankform.pdf

- The Importance of Play in Promoting Healthy Child Development and Maintaining Strong Parent-Child Bonds (281 KB)
  www.aap.org/pressroom/playFINAL.pdf

- Hospital Guidelines for Pediatrics in Disasters (917 KB)
  Available from: http://www.nyc.gov/html/doh/html/bhpp/bhpp-focus-ped.shtml#1

- Pediatric Disaster Preparedness in the Wake of Katrina: Lessons to be Learned (108 KB)
  www.aap.org/disasters/pdf/PDP-in-the-Wake-of-Katrina.pdf

Resources for Children's Social Services

While not an all-inclusive list, the following websites and documents will help professionals in children's social services when planning for the unique needs of children in disasters. Also see the Resources for Children page.

Web Links

- American Red Cross Disaster Preparation Training
  http://www.redcross.org/services/prepare/0,1082,0_239_,00.html

- Camp Noah
  http://www.campnoah.org

- Child Welfare Information Gateway: Disaster Preparedness
  http://www.childwelfare.gov/highlights/disaster/prepare.cfm

- Church World Service Emergency Response Program, Disaster Recovery Help
  http://www.disasterrecoveryhelp.org

- Community Arise Training Curriculum
  http://www.cwserp.org/ (Click Resources, then Community Arise)

- Disaster Response TeenCorps
  http://www.allthingsnewministry.org/drtc.html

- God's Can Do Kids and Renew U Curriculum
  http://www.ldr.org/care/children.html

- Tips for Talking About Disasters
  http://mentalhealth.samhsa.gov/cmhs/EmergencyServices/after.asp

Downloadable Documents

- Coping with Disasters: A Guidebook to Psychosocial Intervention (251 KB)
  www.mhwwb.org/CopingWithDisaster.pdf

- Coping with Disasters and Strengthening Systems: A Framework for Child Welfare Agencies (1,009 KB)
  www.nwtemc.org/documents/copingwithdisasters.pdf

- FEMA Publications Catalog (284 KB)
  http://www.fema.gov/doc/library/femapubcatalog.rtf

- Help in Child Welfare Legal and Judicial System Responses to Children and Families Affected by Disasters (48 KB)
  www.abanet.org/child/disasters.pdf

- Tips for Managing and Preventing Stress: A Guide for Emergency and Disaster Response Workers
  http://mentalhealth.samhsa.gov/cmhs/Katrina/workers.asp

- What Happened to MY World? Helping Children Cope with Natural Disaster and Catastrophe Participant Manual (970 KB)
  Available from: http://www.mercycorps.org/publications/11846

- What Happened to MY World? Helping Children Cope with Natural Disaster and Catastrophe Facilitator's Guide (2,077 KB)
  Available from: http://www.mercycorps.org/publications/11857

Resources for Parents and Caregivers

While not an all-inclusive list, the following websites and documents will help parents and other caregivers when planning for the unique needs of children in disasters. Also see the Resources for Children page.

Web Links

- American Academy of Pediatrics: Children & Disasters
  http://www.aap.org/disasters/families.cfm

- American Red Cross Disaster Preparation Training
  http://www.redcross.org/services/prepare/0,1082,0_239_,00.html

- American Red Cross Masters of Disaster® Family Kit
  http://www.redcross.org/preparedness/familymodule/fam-cd-front-page-1.html

- Camp Noah
  http://www.campnoah.org

- Church World Service Emergency Response Program, Disaster Recovery Help
  http://www.disasterrecoveryhelp.org

- Disaster Response TeenCorps
  http://www.allthingsnewministry.org/drtc.html

- The Dougy Center for Grieving Children and Families
  http://www.dougy.org/

- Emergency Preparedness for Teachers, Students, and Families
  http://readyclassroom.discoveryeducation.com/

- Helping Children After a Natural Disaster: Information for Parents and Teachers
  http://www.nasponline.org/resources/crisis_safety/naturaldisaster_ho.aspx

- Preparing for Disaster: The Parent View
  http://www.naccrra.org/for_parents/coping/disaster.php

- FEMA Resources

  - Ready America
    http://www.ready.gov/america

  - Ready America (Spanish)
    http://www.listo.gov/america

  - The Institute for Business & Home Safety
    http://www.disastersafety.org/

  - Tips for Talking About Disasters
    http://mentalhealth.samhsa.gov/cmhs/EmergencyServices/after.asp

  - Independent Study Course: IS-7 A Citizen's Guide to Disaster Assistance
    http://www.training.fema.gov/EMIWeb/IS/is22.asp

  - Independent Study Course: IS-22 Are You Ready? An In-depth Guide to Citizen Preparedness
    http://training.fema.gov/EMIWeb/IS/is7.asp

  - Independent Study Course: IS-394.a Protecting Your Home or Small Business From Disaster
    http://training.fema.gov/EMIWeb/IS/IS394A.asp

- Resources for Parents and Teachers
  http://www.fema.gov/kids/teacher.htm

Downloadable Documents

- 4 Steps to Prepare Your Family for Disasters (242 KB)
  www.aap.org/family/frk/fourstepsFRK.pdf

- Are You Ready? An In-depth Guide to Citizen Preparedness (21,581 KB)
  Available in English and Spanish from: http://www.fema.gov/areyouready/

- Helping Children Cope with Disaster (488 KB)
  Available in English and Spanish from: http://www.fema.gov/rebuild/recover/cope_child.shtm

- The Importance of Play in Promoting Healthy Child Development and Maintaining Strong Parent-Child Bonds (281 KB)
  www.aap.org/pressroom/playFINAL.pdf

- Know the Rules... Safety Tips for Children Displaced in Natural Disasters and Their Caregivers (153 KB)
  Available in English and Spanish from:
  http://www.missingkids.com/missingkids/servlet/ResourceServlet?LanguageCountry=en_US&PageId=2118

- Listen, Protect, and Connect: Psychological First Aid for Children, Parents, and Other Caregivers After Natural Disasters (184 KB)
  Available from: http://www.cincinnatichildrens.org/svc/alpha/s/school-crisis/psych-aid.htm

- Publications available for purchase from Channing Bete Company®
  http://www.channingbete.com

    o Family Emergency Preparedness: A Presentation Kit

    o Helping Children Cope with Disaster: A Parent and School Staff Handbook

    o How Prepared Is Your Family for an Emergency? A Launch & Learn (CD)

    o Preparing Children for Emergencies – What Parents Need to Know

- Resilience for Kids and Teens: A Guide for Parents and Teachers (385 KB)
  Available from: http://www.apahelpcenter.org/featuredtopics/feature.php?id=39

- Sesame Street, Let's Get Ready! Magazine for Parents and Caregivers (1,213 KB)
  Available in English and Spanish from: http://www.sesameworkshop.org/initiatives/emotion/ready

- What's the Plan? Parent Brochure by NACCRRA (2,373 KB)
  Available from: http://www.naccrra.org/for_parents/coping/disaster

Resources for Children

The following are some websites and books designed especially for children, to help them prepare for and cope with disasters.

Web Links

- Disaster Response TeenCorps
  http://www.allthingsnewministry.org/drtc.html

- Sesame Street Let's Get Ready!
  http://www.sesamestreet.org/ready

- Sesame Street ¡Preparémonos!
  http://www.sesamestreet.org/preparemonos/

- FEMA Resources

  - FEMA for KIDS
    http://www.fema.gov/kids/

  - Ready Kids
    http://www.ready.gov/kids

  - Ready Kids (Spanish)
    http://www.listo.gov/ninos

Downloadable Documents

- The Adventures of the Disaster Twins (1,875 KB)
  Available in English and Spanish from: http://www.fema.gov/kids/twins/

- Can Do and the Storm (6,742 KB)
  Available from: http://www.thecandoduck.com/

- Herman, P.I.C., and the Hunt for a Disaster-proof Shell (480 KB)
  Available from: http://www.fema.gov/kids/herman/

- My Hurricane Story (3,665 KB)
  Available from: http://www.mercycorps.org/publications/11851

- Publications available for purchase from Channing Bete Company®
  http://www.channingbete.com

  o Family Emergency Preparedness: A Presentation Kit

  o Helping Children Cope with Disaster: A Parent and School Staff Handbook

  o How Prepared Is Your Family for an Emergency? A Launch & Learn (CD)

  o Preparing Children for Emergencies – What Parents Need to Know

- Sesame Street Children's Activity Book (2,594 KB)
  Available in English and Spanish from: http://www.sesameworkshop.org/initiatives/emotion/ready

List of Voluntary Agencies

The following is a list of organizations that may provide for the needs of children in disasters. A complete listing of National Voluntary Organizations Active in Disasters is available from http://www.nvoad.org/.

This list is **not** intended to be all-inclusive. You should also check for local organizations that may exist in your area. American Red Cross
http://www.redcross.org

- Brethren Children's Disaster Services
  http://www.brethren.org/site/PageServer?pagename=serve_childrens_disaster_services

- Church World Service Emergency Response Program
  http://www.disasterrecoveryhelp.org

- KaBOOM!
  http://kaboom.org/

- Habitat for Humanity
  http://www.habitat.org

- Mercy Corps
  http://www.mercycorps.org

- National Center for Missing and Exploited Children
  http://www.missingkids.com

- North American Mission Board: Southern Baptist Disaster Relief
  http://www.namb.net/site/c.9qKILUOzEpH/b.224451/k.A400/Disaster_Relief.htm

- The Salvation Army
  http://www.salvationarmyusa.org

- Save the Children
  www.savethechildren.org

You can also download the most current list of National Voluntary Organizations Active in Disasters (VOAD) members here:

- National VOAD Members Resource Directory
  http://www.nvoad.org/Members/NationalMembers/AboutOurMembers/tabid/93/Default.aspx

Acknowledgements

Representatives from the following organizations provided valuable input during the development of the IS 366 course, *Planning for the Needs of Children in Disasters*:

- Save the Children
- The American Red Cross
- The International Association of Emergency Managers
- The American Academy of Pediatrics

Many of the resources listed separately in this Toolkit contributed information and photos for the course. Additional information was provided by the following sources.

- American Academy of Pediatrics: Emergency Preparedness for Children with Special Health Care Needs
  http://www.aap.org/advocacy/epoverview.htm

- *Be Child Care Aware*
  http://www.lsuagcenter.com/en/family_home/family/childcare/be_child_care_aware/

- Children's Defense Fund Reports on Katrina's Children
  http://www.childrensdefense.org/helping-americas-children/special-projects-helping-children-in-need/

- *Emergency Child Care in Mississippi Gets Parents Back to Work*
  http://www.savethechildren.org/emergencies/us/us-gulf-coast-hurricanes/emergency-child-care-in-mississippi-gets-parents-back-to-work.html

- Gurwitch, R. H., Pfefferbaum, B., Montgomery, J. M., Klomp, R. W., & Reissman, D. B. (2007). Building community resilience for children and families. Oklahoma City: Terrorism and Disaster Center at the University of Oklahoma Health Sciences Center
  www.nctsnet.org/nctsn_assets/pdfs/edu_materials/BuildingCommunity_FINAL_02-12-07.pdf

- *Introduction to Emergency Management*. Second Edition. Haddow, George and Jane Bullock. Elsevier. Burlington, MA. 2006 (no Web link available)

- Laudon, Kenneth C., and Laudon Jane P. 2000. *Management Information Systems*, 6th Edition, Prentice Hall Publishing Company: Upper Saddle River, NJ (no Web link available)

- Press Release, "National Center for Missing & Exploited Children Reunites Last Missing Child Separated by Hurricane Katrina and Rita." March 17, 2006.
  http://www.missingkids.com/missingkids/servlet/NewsEventServlet?LanguageCountry=en_US&PageId=2317

- Project Rebuild Plaquemines
  http://www.projectrebuildplaquemines.org/

- Save the Children Video Clip: Safe Spaces (Child Friendly Spaces)
  Available for viewing at: http://www.savethechildren.org/programs/us-programs/safe-spaces-us.html

- Save the Children's "Ten Tips to Help Children Cope with Disaster."
  http://www.savethechildren.org/emergencies/us/us-gulf-coast-hurricanes/helping-children-cope-with-disaster.html

- Terrorism and Disaster Center at University of Oklahoma Health Sciences Center
  http://www.oumedicine.com/body.cfm?id=3737
- United States Government Accountability Office Testimony: Emergency Management: Status of School Districts' Planning and Preparedness
  Available for download from: www.gao.gov/new.items/d07821t.pdf
- Up, Up and Away! MeritCare Patient Story
  http://www.meritcare.com/medicalservices/specialties/childrens/PatientStories/ViewStory.aspx?id=37

FEMA EMI would also like to extend special thanks to the following individuals for allowing us to tell their stories:

- Charles, Lisa, Cortez, and family ("The Children of Katrina and Rita")
- Danielle and son, Jackson ("A Hospital's Disaster Readiness is Put to the Test")
- Valerie and family ("A Narrow Escape")
- Heather Ordover and former students at the High School for Leadership and Public Service in New York City ("In Their Words: High School Students Reflect on 9/11")

www.ingramcontent.com/pod-product-compliance
Lightning Source LLC
Chambersburg PA
CBHW081855280526
45789CB00007B/2706